THE GREAT WORKPLACE 2.0:

It's Not How Big You Are, It's How Remarkable

By Robert A. Schepens, CPC

Cover design by Jim Park
Layout and design by Kaelyn Hrabak
Edited by Randy Wood

ISBN: 978-0-9839983-8-9

LCCN: 2013930023

Contents

Dedication

I dedicate this book to myself. I did the research, sat in a film studio for over 500 hours, skipped many lunches, dinners and *"coffees"* with other CEOs, suffered some real fools, stayed up nights and wrote the whole darn thing myself. Why should I say thanks to anyone? I did the work.

Okay, this time for real:

This work is dedicated to our *"Champions"* at Champion Personnel System, a truly Remarkable Organization with Remarkable people. They allowed me the peace of mind to write during business hours while they lived the 13 characteristics of The Great Workplace 2.0.

I also dedicate this work to my beautiful and Remarkable wife Marti, an enrolled Seminole-Creek Native American who *"voluntarily"* and with *"great sacrifice"* went shopping most weekends to give me alone-time to write. You are welcome my dear Wife. American Express called and wants to speak with you.

To Randy Wood, my editor, you showed me that a Valparaiso/UCLA/John Carroll/Cambridge education was meaningless in front of a keyboard. Darn, you are good.

And to the more than 500 CEOs, managers and senior human resource professionals I have met with and talked to over many years. You endured through direct and chaotic questioning, came through with interesting answers and inspired me in so many ways. May all of you see yourselves in this work, directly or indirectly.

Mostly I dedicate this book to my father, Ralph A. Schepens, founder of Champion Personnel. You didn't have time to write your book, but you had the time to teach me that *"Second Best Isn't Good Enough."* Thanks, Dad. This is my gift back to you and Mom.

Foreword
By Mark Hauserman

Why Read This?

Most of the business-related books you may have read rely on larger corporations for the data that formed the conclusions found in the lessons provided by their case studies. This technique assures an adequate quantity of data points, but also drives the research toward larger organizations such as Fortune 1000 companies. These companies typically have 10,000 employees or more (2008 Census). While we can learn a lot from Walmart, who regained their status as America's largest company last year, your association with Walmart will probably be through buying your office supplies from their Sam's Club subsidiary.

Statistically, chances are excellent that you either run or work for a smaller enterprise. If this description fits you, or you work for a larger organization and are looking for ways to be better, this book is for you.

At a recent meeting of business owners, I asked: *"How many of you are doing what you did five years ago?"* Not one hand went up.

If you want to cope more effectively with the change that is happening all around you, The Great Workplace will provide the tools to build a sustainable strategy to protect and leverage the hard work you have already accomplished.

How do I acquire the lessons to get the result?

The Great Workplace 2.0 is a *'how-to"* for shaping your enterprise into one that is world class.

From the first chapter, the author develops the process, starting with the Tipi. A Native American himself, the author uses the symbolism of the Tipi, as an analogy for The Great Workplace. Did you know that the Tipi has actually been used by dozens of peoples for thousands of years around the world and yet will help you to understand how The Great Workplace is built? This is the first lesson of the book: Not everything that is *"new"* is really *"new"*.

Each chapter starts with an executive summary. Why other authors have not adopted this technique is beyond me. It not only conserves your time, it helps you to focus on the information that is most important to you now and will let you return to it later as you execute your plans.

The chapters have themes, and more importantly, definition of what they are; *"collaboration"* for example and how to embed it in your enterprise. Along the way, you will learn not only what it is, but what it is not. Collaboration, for example, is not an event, it is a process. It is not only internal, but also external. It is the wellspring of innovation and creativity. It extends the reach of the owner, leveraging your time and results.

Mom and apple pie, right? Think this is too obvious for you? Then ask yourself what your game plan is to install, improve and measure collaboration in your organization?

Many books have some or all of this information, but our author ramps it up for you by providing the tools you can use to make your own implementation plan. He does not try to outguess your strategy, but supports it by encouraging you to select the components that are most critical to your enterprise to work on.

Confident or Cocky?

Why would you think that all this stuff is good stuff?

Being an entrepreneur has become a badge of honor. People who probably know little about being one are not hesitant about discussing the finer points of what makes them successful.

Robert could probably depend on the hard-earned lessons of operating his own companies for over 30 years and just start preaching to you. But like any good business owner, he wanted to test his hypothesis in the field. He also wanted to capture the lessons from other successful entrepreneurs to see what was in their stew. He conducted in-depth interviews with many of Northeast Ohio's most successful business owners. A recap of this process is in the introduction, but it says something about the author. Many books, which are sold by clever marketing campaigns, are about: *"How Mr. X built BigCorp into a world-class business."* I love these stories because their subtitles usually should be: *"Just before his successor sold the company that was on an unsustainable path."*

The test of greatness is nearly always time. This measure works for most things including: art, music, literature and business. The Muldoon Center for Entrepreneurship at John Carroll University each year gives two awards. One of them, The John J. Kahl, Sr. award for Creative Leadership, recognizes individuals who have distinguished themselves by the sustained application of creative leadership to their businesses or organizations over a substantial period, resulting in above-average growth and improvement.

While we do not have a specific timeframe in mind, most of the winners have successfully run their organizations for over 20 years.

Even Robert's own success was not enough to guarantee that The Great Workplace 2.0 had the right stuff. He got the best-in-class business leaders to share their ideas on what has made them so successful and incorporated it into the book.

Our Elevator Speech

If you are a publisher, or an inveterate reader, you will recognize this as the abridged version of a foreword. I have told you what I wanted to and your time is too important for me to rewrite the book in the foreword, but I guess I should say something about Robert and myself.

Robert Schepens is the owner of several highly successful companies. A Native American, he is active in the preservation of American Indian heritage, both participating in tribal ceremonies and counseling tribes on business practices.

He is a student of business. Interviewing hundreds of people about what made them successful is not a Saturday afternoon job. He has spent thousands of hours over a number of years. The reason he has been so successful getting time-challenged business owners to sit for interviews is his knowledge of the topic and real interest in what they have to say. I recently read that: *"salesmen who make $50,000 listen 25% of the time, salesmen who make $500,000 listen 75% of the time."* This is Robert. He doesn't finish your sentences for you and he is genuinely interested in your thoughts.

I am the Director of the Muldoon Center for Entrepreneurship at John Carroll University. This is a second career, after spending over 20 years running my own companies, some successfully.

I am fortunate to have landed in a Jesuit university, where academic discipline is a part of the DNA. I also benefitted from the opportunity to work with an amazing team of educators, who, unlike me, actually know what good teaching is all about.

Starting from scratch to create a program that focuses on Arts and Sciences undergraduates as well as business students, the innovative Minor in Entrepreneurship at John Carroll was recently recognized as the top undergraduate entrepreneurship program in Ohio and #18 in the United States by Bloomberg BusinessWeek.

Complementing the Minor is a group of programs that enable students to spread their wings with the help of the John Carroll Entrepreneurs Association, a peer group of over 200 Northeast Ohio business owners, Robert included, who add a dose of reality to their education.

I could go another couple of paragraphs thanking people, but, like the Oscars, I believe my 45 seconds is up.

Preface

I have been a professional recruiter and business owner the majority of my adult life. I have also held professional-level positions in Human Resources, Marketing, Sales and Corporate Outplacement. In that time I have become intimate with a thousand business organizations and all personnel levels from the chairman's office to the Human Resources suite. I have led divisions of medium-sized companies that grew dramatically, studied other companies doing the same, and was saddened when entrepreneurs failed. I have grown my own business dramatically, and in so doing established new benchmarks and made a few god-awful mistakes. I have witnessed the good, the bad and the Remarkable. And, I have learned a few things on my way.

In 2002, I and several other creative people started a project called *"A Job Near Home."* It began as a Job Board for Northeast Ohio. The uniqueness of this concept was that it would have content interesting to hiring authorities and entrepreneurs. We created a video section to the website, with several *"channels,"* built a four-camera, high-definition studio and started filming interviews with business owners, executives and social entrepreneurs.

The video channels were titled: Entrepreneur to Entrepreneur (E2E), People Making a Difference in Northeast Ohio and Innovation NEO. Over 300 interesting people sat with me for hours in front of four professional video and audio folks while I dug and mined for their Success Factors and Insights into why and how these Remarkable people made a difference to organizations. Hundreds more good people were interviewed off-camera or suffered bad coffee with me squeezed into their normal business schedules. With the interviews, I devoured over 250 business books from Barnes and Noble bookshelves, Half-Priced Bookstore and eventually began mining the Kindle/ Amazon store to compare findings.

I also continued to meet with prospects and clients for my main business, Champion Personnel System, Inc. During this time Champion achieved multiple Weatherhead 100 Awards, multiple NorthCoast 99 Awards along with several national and local recognitions for excellence and customer satisfaction. We also achieved ISO 9001:2000 registration.

I was learning that there was simply something different in how small- to medium-sized businesses attained success, different than what is typically written in best-seller books about the big companies like GE, Microsoft and Boeing. What I had read in these big company books was frankly difficult to impossible to duplicate in the smaller business. And, being more than just curious, I started digging for the commonalities of their success.

I started writing articles about my findings for our The Great Workplace.com website, which grew our site's traffic to over 100,000 unique visitors annually world-wide.

Feeling the recession coming on in 2008, we astutely put the launch of A Job Near Home.com on hold. But I continued my

"What, How and Why?" interrogations of business owners and executives, anytime, anywhere I could get them.

At some point I thought of compiling those Remarkable findings and articles into a book, which sounded like a LOT of work. Then I was approached by the publisher of Smart Business Magazine, Dustin Klein, and I began to take the prospect seriously.

Dustin and my editor, Randy Wood of Black Cat Creative Services, convinced me that a book project was worth the effort and would add value to the market. And so it started. It has been a Remarkable journey and hopefully you will feel the same about our findings.

Be Remarkable. It is worth your journey.

"Participant" in
The Great Workplace 2.0 Defined

In The Great Workplace 2.0, we use a term not typically used within *"Legacy"* (old model) organizations. The term is Participant. It is purposefully used to define the change in attitude and status toward those people and organizations that participate in an organization's success, or failure.

The underlying question in this definition is: *"How does the organization treat vendors, contractors and potential employees, compared to how they treat customers?"* The assumption is that customers are treated VERY well as customers define the revenue and future for the organization.

Ever walk into a company for an appointment and been treated like the proverbial red-haired stepchild by the company greeter or another employee (Always)? You instantly feel like you are not wanted, regardless of what you could do for the organization. You KNEW you were excluded. Everyone there wears a Blue Jersey and yours is Yellow,.

The foundation of The Great Workplace is qualitatively one of Inclusion. Legacy organizations typically practice true Inclusion only among defined internal Groups or around the Status of individuals. *"Outsiders"* are, well, outsiders.

The Great Workplace 2.0 has redefined the perceived status of the people and organizations that help move it forward with a more inclusive attitude (Environment) and level of appreciation. They have changed the way they describe, refer to and treat those who touch the organization (*"Stakeholders"*, Employees, Vendors, Board, Applicants, Contractors, Freelancers, Potential Vendors, Customers and Surrounding Community) and redefined their status to be *"Participants."*

"Participant" purposefully elevates all people, organizations and community that touch the organization to jersey-wearing players, and as such bestows a level of accountability and ownership to them to coincide with their inclusion. If you wear the jersey, if you touch the ball or protect it, you have a sense of accountability. You are in the game and can influence its outcome. In legacy organizations, you knew your status; you were on the inside or you were out of the command and control loop, and the organization let you know it with certainty, sometimes with impunity, sometimes at a minimal level, until your *"Touch"* was no longer needed. As a matter of fact, in legacy organizations, the internal folks were (are) trained and encouraged to treat outsiders as challengers. You didn't dare get too close to a vendor or other outsider.

By contrast, The Great Workplace 2.0 recognizes that Participants bring special, valuable and unique knowledge to the game, and the winning the game is all about utilizing that special knowledge or at the very least the optimal use of general knowledge. The Great Workplace 2.0 recognizes that in the business world of today,

"Partners" and *"Collaborators"* in many ways know more about the market the organization is part of than either the organization itself, or groups within the organization.

It recognizes that any Participant holds knowledge the organization needs and instead of simply bidding for and buying it, The Great Workplace 2.0 encompasses that value by inclusion. Inclusion maintains dialogue and dialogue increases networking, idea exchange and innovation. It is also called Collaboration: disparate purposes uniting for a single purpose.

In a Legacy workplace Inside is just that: select participants are part of the insiders group, membership therein being somewhat subjective if not defined, and therefore deemed valuable. The concept of an Outsider is fostered to validate or enhance the status of the Insiders and to create a sense of value to those residing inside.

Outsiders, regardless of their potential contribution to the organization's success, walk in with a built-in *"want"* of value. They can never be quite what an insider is. They are spectators and water boys and are rarely allowed to *"wear the jersey."* They are constantly on *"probation"* and their status is only as good as the mood of the contact. They are task doers and expendable when the timing suits the inner circle.

"Inside Value" has been created in many ways due to the lack of a greater Purpose attached to the work of ANY person or group having influence with the organization.

Legacy workplaces have been particularly adept at creating an Us-versus-Them environment. It can be seen and felt by any outsider, but especially by those who have become new Insiders. They instantly feel a value they have not earned, but have had bestowed upon them due to their change in status. A person who was a vendor, who then becomes an employee, suddenly becomes a trusted *"Insider"* member. Not long before, that same person was left to wait one hour in the lobby even though they were on time for their appointment.

The Great Workplace 2.0 has simply grown to maturity faster than the Legacy workplace. Their environment, training, leadership and culture is geared toward treating all people engaged in the workplace as valued members working toward the success of that organization, right down to the person who answers the phone and greets visitors. After all, a true measure of the culture of an organization and the measure of their future success is whether the organization treats potential Participants as well as they treat customers, or even better.

Mistakes: Treating a vendor as a nonperson or an organization as though they were only interested in your money won't fly in the marketplace. If your representatives were treated that way when they are creating value for your customers through delivering your organization's purpose, you would not do business with that customer for very long. A well-regarded and included vendor may (and probably does) know something you do not. They may intersect with your current Innovation initiatives and move those forward where you cannot.

Treat a job candidate like an inmate at an interrogation camp. Fail to answer their good questions, and have them spend countless hours being *"interviewed"* by your lowest HR person, who has no clue what the job being interviewed for is or what objectives the person will be expected to accomplish. Make a good candidate wait for 30 minutes in the lobby with other candidates so they will feel summoned to a *"Cattle Call"* after they leave two hours later. And, don't tell them anything about why they should want to work there. They probably don't have a network of good people.

Treat the community with suspicion and contempt. Don't get involved. After all, they just want your money. No one in the area will ever want to work for you.

The Great Workplace way:
Crawl out of your three-foot circle. ANYONE you meet could offer something to your success. But you won't know who until you are encouraging, civil and show respect for others.

Train your *"public contacts"* to be open (to the point confidentiality will allow) and not act as though they are Castle Guards. That includes your people in supply chain, Human Resources, management, reception, controller, owner, and anyone involved in networking. Without training, the average person somehow believes it is their job to be cold, pompous and uninviting (they may be scared). The people who work with any outsider need to know that your organization's reputation, that you spent big money on developing, could be trashed in one sentence by an insensitive attitude.

Great Workplace examples:
When I show up for an appointment as a Recruiter or invited Consultant:

Receptionist: *"Hello Mr. Schepens, Mr. Jones is expecting you. Jim is running a little late for your meeting, but will be with you very soon. Could I get you coffee or water?"*

My impression: I am valued. I am treated with respect and am now very enthusiastic to do the same with everyone I meet. I may offer free advice, better pricing or a lead. I am valued.

(Jones told the Receptionist that a *"Mr. Schepens"* would be here at 2:00 for a meeting. Simple info to convey).

Purchasing Person: *"Mr. Schepens, thank you for meeting with us. We have looked at your information, website, and I can tell you we are very interested in learning what you know."* Or, *"In what ways do you believe you can help ABC company?"* Or: *"What can we tell you about ABC company and our specific requirements or needs?"* Civil, respectful, open, Collaborative (Purchasing guy wants to know true value, not just price, and will, with an encouraging attitude, let you take your best shot).

Owner/ Chief: *"Robert, let me tell you about our corporate Vision for the future, and find out if there is any value to BOTH of us in a future meeting? What I am looking for is an organization that will bring more value to us than we bring money to them. What can you provide to us that we cannot get elsewhere?"* (With an encouraging smile). The Owner knows how he wants to be treated, and is also smart enough to know you are probably talking with other people in his industry or potentially his customers. He/she might be busy, but will act as though you are the ONLY person he is interested in right now. It has been said that former President Bill Clinton could make anyone feel that important. Good reputation to have, especially when you have a reputation to correct.

"Participant" rather than outsider, contractor or vendor, is a term of inclusion that allows people to wear your jersey or carry your tribal flag, and want to contribute.

In the Tipi, the visitor is always fed, given a seat of honor at the fire, and listened to with intent. That holds today in traditional families, in apartments and homes. It is called Respect. Years ago, I was privileged to meet with Cherokee Nation Chief, Dr. Wilma Mankiller. I was selling insurance to the Nation. Each person I met with before Dr. Mankiller was inviting. When she entered the conference room, she sat next to me, not at the head of the rather large table. We chatted about inconsequential things like strangers do. Then she said: *"We'll talk about business in a few minutes. What I really want to know is who are YOU as a person?"* About 20-minutes later, she nodded to an assistant and told her to cancel her other morning appointments, she was taking me on a personal tour of the Reservation. I had not mentioned anything about being connected to the Native community in Cleveland. During the car-tour and stopping at a few homes and businesses, we talked about insurance and what my company could do for her people. She needed to know we could achieve the Nation's Management Purpose and goals. Upon parting later that morning she said: *"You have Native ancestors don't you?"* Honestly, I look very much like a non-native guy, three-piece suit and all. She was very perceptive to see what was inside me, not just at the bottom line I was offering.

The Tipi as the Symbol of The Great Workplace:
The Enduring Organization, Shared Common Purpose

Executive Summary:
- Long before today and the business plan, the groundwork for a strong presence was created by people seeking leadership and the desire to belong, or the desire to represent that they belong.
- The duty of Leadership is in the re-creation of this fundamental connectedness.
- The Tipi and what it represents for The Great Workplaces is analogous to this duty.

There is a true purpose in representing an organization not as a pyramid, as used in so many business books, but as a Tipi. Tipis are for the living, where pyramids are for those whom have passed. A pyramid is heavy, rigid and closed. A Tipi is light, portable and open. A pyramid glorifies one individual; a Tipi represents a Tribal or Nation-Connection.

The Great Workplaces have created their own Tipis, their Shared Culture (Values in action), their Shared Future and their

Shared Language. They create Shared iconic representations of their "Nations" (brands). They create Pride. They Endure.

The Tipi is Remarkable

Tipis are most recognized as part of Native American Plains culture, but they are also part of Nordic culture. Lavvu is the Saami equivalent of Tipi. The Saami people, also known as Lapplanders, live above the Arctic Circle in an area known as Sapmi. They are resident in and came before several different Nordic cultures and nations.

How does a Tipi work as an analogy to The Great Workplace? A Tipi is held up by supporting poles arranged at the base in a circle, set far apart, that converging at the top of the structure in a Collaborative fashion; they support each other and the structure itself, never losing their own identity while working for the overall Purpose. The Tipi is a 3-dimensional structure. It is physically solid, but movable. It is flexible according to the Purpose needed. It is iconic and representative of what is inside and the larger organization of which it is a component.

And so it is in The Great Workplace: separate components (divisions, business or operating plans, participants) of an organization all meet in one place (the Collaboration and Purpose) to provide a substantial structure to the whole. Teamwork and Collaboration provide the structure, but an Integrated Business Plan is at the top (Convergence). For visual reference, many Tipis have a circular "collar" at the very top, which holds the poles in order and balances the entire structure, with Purpose. That is the Integrated Business Plan, and the entire structure becomes Enduring.

Tipis are very portable (Fluid), and very iconic. Each family unit decorates their structure with meaningful symbols that identify the residents, tribe and nation or spirit guides. A flag of the Nation, Tribe, Clan or family can be flown atop the Tipi to further identify the residents.

Tipis are not mere lodgings, but sacred places for the members. Extended family members can live or gather there, as well as valued animals (horses; the equivalent in business organizations today might be Vendors, Contractors or other Participants). Guests are given food and shelter, and treated with great respect. In many Native cultures, council meetings, today's equivalent: Board of Directors, other Tribes (Vendors) and even rival tribe members (competitors) meet to make decisions or to trade.

Inside the center of the Tipi is a fire pit, where living warmth is generated, cooking is done, and gatherings are accomplished. It is also a place to acknowledge thanks to the spirits and The Creator. The Tipi is open at the top to allow smoke to exit, cool air to come in, and to allow the residents a direct line to The Creator.

To Native people, the Circle of Life (today's economic tribal equivalent: business cycles, the flow of organizational development, succession planning, the circle of communications in an organization) is seen in all things, including the circle in which the Tipi structure is built.

This circle is not by chance, but by design. All things and all lives are connected. Mitakuye Oyasin, which is Lakota-Sioux for *"We are all related."*

The Great Workplaces of today are, by my evaluation, *"Tribal"* in nature, as are most human affinity groups. People want and need to identify with an affinity group; a group of people with whom they have, or want to have common interests and experiences. We are drawn to those people and organizations.

We seek them and support them. Belonging to something larger than ourselves, with a greater Purpose, gives us confidence and nurtures our inner needs. Becoming a recognized part of something larger can produce the conditions under which Good People achieve Great Results.

It is why people in Los Angeles will wear NY Yankee jerseys: they want to identify in some way with the characteristics they believe that group has, even though they don't have a physical connection. Those LA folks seek the affinity. It most cases the desire to connect cannot be explained logically. It is a belief or conviction. It lifts and inspires.

Becoming *"Tribal"* as a Workplace means that the participants Share a Common Purpose, Values and Identity with (Purpose, Values, Vision, Goals) and have voluntarily aligned with the Visible and Tangible characteristics of that organization.

Within sovereign Native Nations, Tribes and Clans, a common language is spoken. Even though there are or were over 500 distinct Native languages within North America.

Within The Great Workplaces, participants have learned and share a Common Language: Values, Purpose, Visions and Missions. A common Language Connects Participants. Without it, a weak *"Nation"* is produced.

This is one of the most critical duties of the Leader or Leader with Credentials; to Visibly, Tangibly walk the talk. To Lead when there is uncertainty. To create the hope of the future. There will be a wealth of warriors to lead a Mission or single charge up the hill. The Leader needs to speak the Common language, so all can learn.

One must simply think of the iconic images of Tecumseh, Sitting Bull, Red Cloud, Chief Joseph, Crazy Horse, Geronimo and Wilma Mankiller to understand that they tangibly represented an intangible: Their Nations, their Tribes, and their common Future. Their Pride. A non-native person may think that these Icons and all they represent have been conquered and therefore are no longer relevant. This is not even close to the truth, Kemosabe (Potawatomi for *"trusted friend."* You know, Tonto and the other guy who rode with him).

Native people endure. I'm not making a political statement here, but after over 500 years of attempts to marginalize each Nation, Tribe and group of people, from the Powhatan and the Wampanoag to the Nez Pierce and the Apache, we are still here and strong.

Here is an example of how and why Nations and people Endure: My wife is *"full-blood"* (enrolled) Oklahoma Seminole-Creek. Her ancestors were forced to walk from Florida to Oklahoma on the Trail of Tears. When asked if she is *"Indian"* she replies proudly: *"No, I am Seminole-Creek."*

The Great Workplaces have created their own Tipis, their Shared Culture (Values in action), their Shared Future and their Shared Language. They create Shared iconic representations of their "Nations" (brands). They create Pride. They Endure.

Do your participants self-identify with your Tribe or Nation? Give them a reason to do so. Make your Tipi Remarkable.

A brief and arguable explanation of the hierarchy of Native cultures: **1)** Nation (ex: Dakota), **2)** Tribe (Mdewakanton) **3)** Clan (Bear, Bird) **4)** Family (Walks with Owl Feathers).

I ask deference from my Native Brothers and Sisters for any misuse of terms and explanations in this workplace analogy, as well as the use of the analogy itself. An Elder once told me that teaching was not only of value but an expectation, and we are never to apologize, I won't either. Ho Hecetuyelo. Mikauyae Oyasin (I have spoken, we are all related. Lakota Oyate language).

The idea of the Tipi as The Great Workplace was not mine alone. That same Elder called my offices: *"Echon (eh-chon) Tipi"*: The Home of Commerce. Elders are wise.

13 Attributes of
The Great Workplace 2.0

"It's not how BIG you are. It's how Remarkable"

The Great Workplace 2.0™ is an ongoing project that began in 2004. The focus of this research has been one-on-one meetings and conversations with business owners, CEOs, C-Level managers and top-level Human Resource executives in small- to medium-sized organizations in Northeast Ohio. We define *"small to medium"* as employing up to about 700 people. Our largest organization interviewed had annual sales volume of about $750 Million. Alternatively, our smallest interviewed organizations employed about 10 full time equivalents. Some startups were part of our base, but most had been in existence for at least 4 years.

About 5 percent of these organizations are non-profit, run by social entrepreneurs functioning in business or community-oriented economic services.

Most of the organizations are already on lists of successful organizations; The Weatherhead 100, North Coast 99, Business Success in Northeast Ohio, The Entrepreneurs Edge, John Carroll University Entrepreneurs Association, referrals from one CEO to another, and of course the clients of the Recruiting and Staffing services with whom I am proud to be associated. This last is particularly noteworthy as we have been able to gather pertinent insight into both Great and Not-So-Great workplaces in an ongoing and intimate fashion. The list of organizations associated with this project totals somewhere north of 500.

It is important to note that personal meetings, follow up phone calls and some casual conversations constitute our findings, not *"fill in the blank"* surveys. Surveys have a habit of being handed off to underlings or filled out with guarded responses. We preferred the method of *"questioning the answer"* to uncover reality versus public relations statements. It is truly gratifying what real information can be discovered and discussed over a cup of coffee, lunch, dinner or in-depth on-camera interview. Add to the list of organizational interviews, the input of professional advisors, highly regarded educators, association managers and business owners of great influence to other business owners, and the base of our research becomes more than significant. It also did not hurt that during this project, I consumed over 250 *"business success"* books. My home library now looks like a haven for budding entrepreneurs.

To their credit, many busy and successful entrepreneurs gave up entire afternoons to not only chat privately about their successes and failures, but sat in a four camera, HD video studio being interviewed on camera ... by me.

One such friend is Ray Dalton, CEO of enormously successful PartsSource Inc., a perennial Weatherhead 100 winner (#1 the year we met). Ray and I met through a friend of mine Doug Brown, a Vice President at PartsSource, at our mutual first Weatherhead 100 Award ceremony (Champion was #50). Doug and I were fortunate to be part of Capitol American Insurance, a super-fast growth company, before it was acquired by Conseco and moved to Indiana (with a good contingency of Capital people at the time). I mention Ray Dalton as his track record has included more than seven successful business ventures and more public awards for creating *"Great"* entrepreneurial organizations. Many people use the term "serial entrepreneur" to describe this achievement.

The list of patient and open CEOs is long. Most continue to be successful, many have not. The content of TGW 2.0 comes not only from successful people and organizations, but also the ones who never quite made it.

I need to insert one *"editorial"* point here: The vast majority of organizations are privately owned or closely held. Privacy is a real and important issue to many owners and CEOs. I have respected their privacy to the letter, and when asked NOT to quote people or use their organizations in an identifiable way, I have stuck to that. Many have said they are not seeking publicity for specifics, or at all.

This work is meant to be a fluid exposé on concepts of core values, working plans, characteristics and strategies that make a great workplace, and how these discovered characteristics are repeatable, duplicate-able and downright critical for any owner, CEO or Manager of a small- to medium-sized organization. Time will also be spent on what not to do, examples of note, and observations of people and plans.

The *"Social Contract"* with employers and workers has changed. The *"workplace"* is no longer just hired employees and employer. It is no longer a space confined to a legacy corporate structure. And that has dramatically changed the way people and executives look at Great Places To Work, and in turn Great Workplaces. The focus, in a highly productive company, has shifted to PURPOSE: both from an individual point of view and a *"corporate viewpoint."* Walls and structures are coming down or are being made visible. Old lines of communications (Such as *"Command and Control"*) have been amended and the concept of *"New Ideas"* is no longer just defined as internal.

The purpose of The Great Workplace 2.0™ is simple: while it is happening, show core changes in Great Workplaces, so that start-ups, small and mid-size companies, can extract the principles that other companies are discovering. By embracing the examples set down here, an organization can develop in a healthy and sustainable fashion and return to our economy great dividends of revenue, value and innovation. By discovering what the small- to mid-sized organization is doing to be Great, we are purposefully showing what can be duplicated by other small- to mid-sized organizations. BIG company success stories are wonderful reading, and great examples, but if you are like me (small company owner) what most of The Big Guys do, we are not able to directly duplicate The big guys have more people in their evening cleaning crews than we do employees and more money in their coffee and beverage budget than we do in our credit lines.

Realistically, being Great or Remarkable is NOT all about size or money, it is about the foundations we create and the Leadership we provide. We create more jobs than the big guys do, and we can feel *"damn proud"* of our accomplishments.

The Great Workplace functions at a higher level of purpose and productivity and is a more interesting place to work than other organizations. It attracts great talent and it attracts great results — for the customer. It extends its intelligent self-interests beyond the executive suite into the depths of its own employment, into the rich treasure troves of vendor knowledge, the community, and to all participants (stake/shareholders). It reaches out to the crowd within its community for opportunities and solutions. A Great Workplace understands intrinsically that being *"open"* is an advantage. When it reaches out, it extends its hand in a positive manner both internally and externally looking for strengths and sustainable principles on which to further develop the business and the opportunities for participants. It simply does not adhere to the old model of corporate hierarchy and held power. A Great Workplace of today invites being benchmarked, but is always one step beyond being so static that its definitions are fluid.

A Great Workplace is in fact a fluid community. It interacts with its Participants and creates communication avenues that foster the immediate interaction of questions, ideas, opinions and therefore opportunities and solutions. It has substantially removed the obstacles to Innovation and discouraged most linear or legacy ideals. It uses knowledge gained through more *"open-invitation"* processes and feeds upon the rich knowledge and input from all sources that touch the organization. It is both created on and by purpose and has the ability to change its tactical or strategic directions quickly, always anchored to its fundamental Purpose. The corporate legacy model focused upon impressive-sounding *"Mission Statements"* and *"Shareholder Return"* (regardless of what that meant). In many circumstances, businesses were operated not because they really wanted to, but because they *"should."* They sustained themselves because there were stock certificates and legacies to support.

That old model was built upon relative size and the ability to do things for itself on a grand scale: benefits, bonuses, unions, giveaways, charitable donations, dividends and having employees see their company in print or in TV ads. If you work for Shell Oil or for General Motors you must work for a great company. We feted big companies as great workplaces because they flowed forth with great benefits, nominally gave away their services as charity and in general treated employees as cats in Pharaoh's chambers. Just the mention of, *"I work for National City Bank,"* meant something impressive. It was akin to saying that you attended Notre Dame while the Fighting Irish were a national football powerhouse. The *"aura"* was the value. The old model created strong bodies of *"paycheck recipients"* and the reputation of those bodies became the mirror of all things corporate. The Great Workplace 2.0 creates powerful *"Tribes"*, based on Shared Purpose and Collective Intelligence, rather than aura. These organizational Tribes practice the language of *"We"* that is born from Values, Purpose and Culture (Values In Action).

It is with great reflection and intent, not just from my personal cultural values, that The Great Workplace is depicted as a Tipi, rather than a one-dimensional pyramid to which so many business books default.

Teamwork is now more important than ever, but only when it has Collaboration at its foundation. Teamwork can be interpreted as a group of similarly trained or deployed people working for a single mission (e.g., basketball players: a linear orientation). Collaboration is geared toward having disparate talents working for a single outcome (even from different geographies), through different purposes that converge.

Collaboration in The Great Workplace 2.0 is secured by Values and tied to the Integrated Business Plan that pulls together Unit plans under a single Purpose, regardless of separate Missions within each unit.

The core issue may be that we are still celebrating and making plans around the old model of great workplaces while the purposeful shift representing what makes a Great Workplace or great place to work has been quietly stealing our best people, their minds and talents, and vendors — just like John Galt in Ayn Rand's Atlas Shrugged.

There is absolutely nothing wrong with a BIG great workplace that employs thousands of people. Our work will show what is happening in and could be happening in the companies that employ 50+ percent of our workers and create new jobs and businesses that aren't in the news or on TV: The Great Workplace 2.0™. Future Fortune 1000 companies may start with only a few people, and they too should be aware of how to create the foundations that will assure success as they grow.

It's not how Big you are. It's how Remarkable. Be Remarkable.

Characteristics of The Great Workplace 2.0

1) **Statement of Purpose:** A great workplace has a meaningful Corporate Statement of Purpose that is the foundation for corporate culture and therefore provides greater meaning to employment, work opportunities and strategy. This statement is driven by the effects the organization has on their customers and the role each participant can play in that directive. Purpose becomes an ethos that creates the very foundation for The Great Workplace 2.0™.

2) **Values:** The ability of a workplace to be great should never rely solely upon being big or rich. Great is a value,

and values can never be bought. Jim Collins in *Built To Last*, defines it this way: *"It is dedicated to the idea that true greatness comes in direct proportion to the passionate pursuit of a purpose beyond money."* Values are CULTURE, and culture is the (mostly) unseen core of what makes the organization a living, breathing entity. Culture is the focal point of intent. We define Culture as *"Values In Action"*.

3) **What, Why, How:** Of the products or services being offered. The "What" is easy. It is the same as your competition, in the eyes of the customer. The Great Workplace combines its Values, Purpose, and therefore Culture into the differentiators of the "How" (what makes your entire offering unique). The "Why" is your ultimate purpose FOR your customer. The Great Workplace doesn't just offer a product or service; it offers an entire package of product/service, company, people and Purpose.

4) **Integrated (Business) Operating Plan:** A great workplace has an operating plan to integrate jobs, careers, participants and the community in their (organizational and individual) pursuit of accomplishing their purpose. Intent or statements are not enough. This operating plan embraces the strategy and tactics of purposeful convergence of knowledge for the participants, and where, how and why obstacles to the purpose can be eliminated or minimized. The IBP merges all individual unit plans into one cohesive and concise set of flexible commands for the organization and its participants as a whole.

5) **The right people doing the right things, right.** A great workplace understands the value of their people. There is a well-thought through consistency of hiring that focuses on properly matching position needs with available talent,

attracting those people, evaluating potential hires, immersing potential participants from first contact and developing talent as it is brought on board. Their hiring methodology goes beyond skill match and years of experience into value-match, potential and a focus on performance-based needs, not just job descriptions.

6) **Tools:** A great workplace provides the tools for all participants to properly execute their responsibilities relative to their assignments and the organization's purpose. *"Tools"* goes beyond mechanical devices and digs deep into development of skills, vision and an orientation to goal-accomplishment.

7) **Immersion:** A great workplace has a working plan for immersion (onboarding) of all participants: (new employees, contractors, vendors, promotions, teams/ groups, community, board, executives, consultants and families). The purpose of this working structure is to reduce the time to productivity and to facilitate the complete engagement of the participant throughout that participant's life cycle.

8) **Collaboration:** A great workplace is committed to fostering a collaborative, productive, engaging and rewarding culture that encompasses customers, prospective employees, employees, vendors, participants and the community. The organization practices collaboration to the extent that *"internal and external"* no longer have a distinction, and it recognizes that "community" has no true boundaries.

9) **Act Local:** A great workplace emphasizes buying locally and promotes its region as a great place to live and work. A great workplace realizes that its core *"family"* extends beyond the factory floor, the cubicles and offices into

the surrounding geography. It realizes and nurtures the reality that an organization and its community are one entity in pursuit of mutual success.

10) **Intelligently Profitable:** A great workplace has a financial focus on being intelligently profitable. This qualitative focus is founded in sustainability, the values within their purpose and a view of intelligent self interest for the organization and all participants. Intelligent self interest is defined as self interest that stands the test of, *"how will my plan affect others?"* It defines who the customer really is.

11) **Management shows and invokes visible, tangible leadership:** This core action directly supports the organization's Statement of Purpose and operating plan. This leadership preserves the integrity of the organization's purpose, and is both duplicate-able and repeatable — at any level.

12) **Transparent Integrity:** A great workplace practices this as a core value. It is the proof of *"Say what you do, do what you say, and prove it"*. For The Great Workplace, Transparent Integrity, allows an inside or outside skeptic to see that public relations and reality match. In essence it says: *"Yes, we really do"*.

13) **Enduring:** A great workplace provides for enterprise sustainability as part of their core culture and is committed to educating all participants about their practices. Sustainability is defined in flexible terms for the organization as a viable entity born from other characteristics of the Integrated Business Plan. Enduring sustainability focuses on the continual existence of the organization as a viable entity for all participants ... today and in the future. The organization's ability to endure

is the result of integrating all planning aspects of the organization's strategy into their IBP. It is the pinnacle of achievement for most organizations.

The above definitions are only a part of an introduction to the entire research results for what makes a The Great Workplace 2.0 of today and tomorrow. The Great Workplace 2.0 is not static. It is updated and changed on a regular basis as we discover other fundamentals that are forming the benchmarks of success. We invite your comments and insights, directly to the author.

One thing that all great workplaces have in common is this: they're **Remarkable** (worthy, noticeable and unique). Not because they have excessive benefits, bonuses, on-site daycare, or a slide that takes you to the ground floor, but because the entire organization has a Purpose that is built around an ideal: Do what's best for the customer.

Purpose in The Great Workplace 2.0:
Touching the Sky, at Ground Level

Executive Summary:
- Purpose is the reason you touch the customer, beyond money, and the reason the customer touches you.
- It is what you do for the customer that causes a customer, to in fact BE a customer.
- Purpose is sustainable and enduring. It is glue. It binds together all parts of the Integrated Business Plan, is the birthplace of core Values and a rally-point for all participants.
- Your Purpose defines why the organization exists now and in the future, and it is laser-targeted at your customer.
- It is different than a Mission Statement in that when a Mission is accomplished it becomes an *"archived entry in history."* Your Purpose has no end.
- Remarkable Organizations not only have a solid and public Purpose, but it is at the core of their existence.

Author's note: *"Purpose"* is at the core of all The Great Workplaces. In this chapter, with intent, I will over-describe

Purpose, refer to many of the other characteristics of the Great Workplace 2.0 which you will read about in subsequent chapters, so to lay the groundwork for the entire concept of The Great Workplace 2.0.

Purpose for the Customer, in all our Great Workplaces, is both a decision and a passion. It resides in the Vision of the leaders and through Engagement with Participants, it becomes Tangible. It is THE reason your organization exists for the Customer, and without it, you could have a series of Missions that will leave a doubt as to WHY and How the organization must perform in ways to please the ultimate decision-maker of your fate: The Customer.

Your Customer is interested in your Purpose, for them. They don't really care about your Missions, for yourself.

Purpose, for an organization and its participants, is an equivalent to (allow me to make this reference with sensitivity) a religious or spiritual belief. In theory it cannot be touched, but you know it is there, and act accordingly.

Purpose, points to and exceeds individual and group objectives and aligns the actions of Participants to the success of your organization.

Purpose, combined with organizational Values, when put into action will produce your Culture. Your Culture will achieve or fall short of your objectives, or Missions. Culture is defined as *"Values in Action"*.

A resonating Purpose answers daily questions from all your participants: *"What should I do now?" "Why are we/I doing this?"* More than any instruction given in training and development of participants, it enhances the instructions with guidance for judgments.

In our chapter *"The Right People Doing the Right Things Right"*, we note that over 60 percent of employees are not engaged in their work. In essence, they work for THEIR reasons, not your organization's reasons. But *"37 percent of US workers are consistently highly engaged in their work"* (Towers Watson Global Workforce Study). A large percentage of those who are highly engaged are both motivated by and identify personally with the higher Purpose of an organization, rather than just the short term Mission. It is a trait I have seen in meetings with Remarkable Organizations, and sorely lacking in those that are not.

From my perspectives as both a Recruiter and an Owner/ Manager of a service that has dealt with over 7,000 hiring organizations, I have found that employees in all career levels, especially The Right People, want their lives, their work and their results to mean something. Something more than helping a company or company owner: *"To become the largest supplier of machined parts in the upper Midwest."*

It is no longer adequate for most individuals to give their time, effort and attention to a thinly veiled *"Mission Statement"* that hides the ultimate pursuit of corporate goals (quarterly earnings reports or stock prices). The typical participant sees right through that and goes to work elsewhere or begins to take advantage of the organization's generosity and focuses on his or her own goals.

The Participants in The Great Workplace want their work efforts to have a Shared Purpose beyond simple material gain, especially when that material gain is for unseen, passive recipients (Shareholders as an example). Working toward a concept or purpose larger or greater than our own self is a touch with immortality. It produces Trust. Those things we do only for ourselves stay within us and perish or dwindle when we focus on the next new shiny thing.

Your Purpose is what will cause Participants to your Success to want to Connect, Engage and Collaborate with you.

The Great Workplaces are evangelical in that way. They seek outwardly and openly for the Right People and the Right Partners. They seek sharing their Purpose with those who can help achieve it.

It is no longer adequate for most individuals to give their time, effort and attention to a thinly veiled *"Mission Statement"* that hides the ultimate pursuit of intrinsic corporate goals (quarterly earnings reports or stock prices). The typical participant sees right through that and goes to work elsewhere or begins to take advantage of the organization's generosity and focuses on his or her own goals.

People work for their reasons (their own Mission focused on themselves, or even their own Purpose if work has none) not yours. And that alone can cause owners to say *"They just don't get it"* about their employees or other participants: Owners/Managers have not given them a reason to *"Get It"*.

There is a marked movement to an ethos based upon common sense and the guiding perspective that in fact, we are all *"in this together, for a REASON"* (Purpose). This realization alone has helped us change from a corporate *"us-versus-them"* mentality which directs insiders against outsiders or insiders versus insiders into using the idea of *"Participants"* to describe ALL people and entities that touch the organization.

Allegorically, your organization's Purpose is where the poles in your Tipi meet and cause your business unit plans to converge. It describes a common Why for those plans and actions.

In Lakota-Sioux culture the phrase, which is also used by many other Native Nations, *"Mitakuye Oyasin"* (Pronounced *"Me-tak-ah-way, O-Yah-Sin"*). It means *"We are all related."* Meaning we share the effects of our actions, both good and not-so good). It defines Shared Purpose. It is a phrase that takes on the qualities of a *"Team Jersey."* It is bigger than each individual, their own Tribe, their own Nation. That phrase is reflected in the uses of a Tipi: a place for all to gather and share.

The Participants in The Great Workplace want their work efforts to have a shared Purpose beyond simple material gain, especially when that material gain is for unseen, passive recipients (Shareholders as an example). Working toward a concept or purpose larger or greater than our own self is a touch with immortality. It produces Connection.

An organization's Purpose is a major reason top talent will choose to be a Participant at one organization over another. Top Talent can work anywhere their skills are needed. But the definition of *"Top Talent"* is changing with the changes of the workplace.

Top talent can choose where, how and why to work with an organization that has a Purpose where they can participate at a higher level than before, and where their lives can take on (new) meanings.

Top talent is now defined as those people who will focus on YOUR purpose, not theirs, first. They know that focusing on the organization's purpose will lead to achieving their goals. In the old model, Top Talent was defined by credentials and skills rather than by Intent and Collaborative attitude.

In a purpose-driven organization, the talent who are focused on their own goals first will be seen as counter-productive and socially out of sync with the community. The word *"Selfish"* will be used to describe their attitude regardless of their skills.

Today's leaders realize that the competitiveness of their product or service is a consequence of the organization's purpose and leadership. Rarely does the product or service itself create Leadership or Purpose.

The Great Workplace 2.0 recognizes that Purpose through an Immersive Culture is not a matter of chance. It is a matter of Touch. Touch is leadership that has created the ability for all participants to see, feel, know and implement the organization's real and stated Purpose.

True Purpose resonates. It has a richness of significance. It has the ability to evoke a shared emotion and belief. People, working together regardless of geography or status, get behind a direction that becomes profitable for everyone involved. People recognize that a group or community with a clear purpose can move mountains that individuals or insulated *"leaders"* cannot. This is what makes the Naval Special Warfare community the most effective in the world (SEALs). Their creed and Purpose resonates in everything they do. It is a brotherhood, even for members who have never met.

True Purpose also invokes the absolute need for *"Visible Tangible Leadership"* and *"Transparent Integrity"* (chapters in The Great Workplace 2.0 and core characteristics), and without the leadership of an organization visibly reflecting in their actions and presence the reality and importance of this Purpose, the organization will and does become not only questionable, but a cause for deep emotional and physical contentiousness (Turnover and half-hearted work efforts).

Both philosophically and in reality, the customer moves the Purpose. It is theirs to move. They move your Purpose so it aligns with their own. The customer is in charge. The customer can be internal or external to the organization (the actual buyer of your purpose on the outside, or any participant to your success on the inside of an organization). In turn, their Purpose can be intrinsic or extrinsic. When their Purpose is extrinsic, you need to know. All participants to your Purpose need to Align it to their own. That is why your Mission Statement does NOT necessarily motivate the external customer. But it can and should motivate and Align your internal Participants for organizational goals.

In ISO-registered quality systems there is a simple phrase used by Quality Guru Randy Cicen of JR Associates in NE Ohio: *"Say what you do, do what you say, and PROVE it."* It is very applicable to Statements of Purpose. Randy has been a leading Quality consultant to service and manufacturing organizations, having guided my own organization to ISO 9001:2000 Registration in 2004.

The NEW Mission Statement: Crafted on Purpose

"It becomes a bad thing when a mission statement devolves into platitudinous pabulum that employees clearly recognize as hypocrisy," writes Darrell Rigby, partner at Bain (quote from *"The Enron Blog"*).

The Great Workplaces are now starting to get it. Organizations that are tuned into participant feedback and public feedback have been feeling the pushback of ego-centric, mistrusted Mission Statements; which are totally organization-centered rather than customer or participant-centered. And, in large part due to that issue, are crafting new *"Mission Statements"* that are more purpose-driven. They have changed their focus on organization milestones (ex: *"Being the BIGGEST in the online banking arena"*) to the results or impacts felt by the ultimate customer (*"Continually making online banking easy for EVERY customer, big or small"*).

Having a *"Mission Statement"* or *"Statement of Purpose"* as a moniker for their ultimate goal is a matter of preference, if there is only one statement to the public with that title. BUT, should the organization prefer to have BOTH (Mission Statement that is internal and time-constrained) then they need to be so titled.

For purposes of internal goal crusades, the Mission Statement is appropriate as well as motivational: *"Become the largest distributor of Plumbing Supplies in Northeast Ohio by December 2015."*

Examples of "Thin" Mission Statements:

These are borrowed from "The Enron Blog" http://caraellison. wordpress.com/2008/08/20/mission-statements-the-good-the-bad-the-terribly-misguided/

To help people and businesses throughout the world realize their full potential. (Microsoft)

Providing solutions in real time to meet our customers' needs. (Halliburton)

ExxonMobil Corporation is committed to being the world's premier petroleum and petrochemical company. To that end, we must continuously achieve superior financial and operating results while adhering to the highest standards of business conduct. These unwavering expectations provide the foundation for our commitments to those with whom we interact. (ExxonMobil)

A website created to help arm the liberty-loving silent majority with ammo — ammo that strikes at the intellectual solar plexus of the Left. (ProtestWarrior.com)

To be the best in the eyes of our customers, employees and shareholders. (American Standard)

"It is our responsibility to assertively administrate timely deliverables in order to solve business problems."
(From the Dilbert Mission Statement Generator)

The New Ventures Mission is to scout profitable growth opportunities in relationships, both internally and externally, in emerging, mission-inclusive markets, and explore new paradigms and then filter and communicate and evangelize the findings."

Yahoo! powers and delights our communities of users, advertisers, and publishers – all of us united in creating indispensable experiences, and fueled by trust."

"Our Mission: Collaborating with partners of government, community-based organizations, communities and the private sector, we provide a community engagement and dialogue clearinghouse."

"To provide capacity training and resources to build individual and collective skills and knowledge in small and large-scale engagement and dialogue processes."

"To convene community engagement and dialogue processes."

"To collect and publish information and best practices of community engagement planning, strategic engagement, organizational renewal and public policy development."

And, if you want to have some fun generating a truly meaningless, business-speak-laden Mission Statement, try this: *http://www.isms.org.uk/mission%20statement.htm*

This site will instantly generate a Mission Statement for your organization like this:

"We will work together to model transparent market share with no increase in price for the benefit of our organization and other private partnerships."

Or this from Laughing Buddha:
http://www.laughing-buddha.net/toys/mission

"We will seamlessly foster enterprise-scale and competitive solutions to meet the needs of an ever-changing marketplace."

Statements of Purpose:

Starbucks: *Our Customers: When we are fully engaged, we connect with, laugh with, and uplift the lives of our customers — even if just for a few moments. Sure, it starts with the promise of a perfectly made beverage, but our work goes far beyond that. It's really about human connection.*

State Farm: *"To educate and build relationships with our current and future customers. To establish and preserve our neighborhoods and schools, and to demonstrate the good neighbor philosophy through our education and safety programs, volunteer efforts and our alliances with many diverse communities."*

Cinecraft (a 70-year old Cleveland leader in film and video, who after 65 years finally landed on their Purpose): *"Telling Stories"*

Champion Personnel System: *"To positively affect our clients' profitability by increasing their workforce productivity."* This is ALL about the client, not about the vendor.

Google Inc. 1998: *"To make it easier to find high-quality information on the web."*

Amazon: *Amazon's vision is to be earth's most customer centric company; to build a place where people can come to find and discover anything they might want to buy online.*

Champion Personnel System (For Clients): *"Make Staffing Easy"* this is a focus on the HR Manager who is, by the nature of their function, exasperated by the need to staff at different levels, at different times, with little or no hassle.

Champion Personnel System (For Job Seekers): *"A Better Job. A Better Life"*

Facebook: *"Facebook's mission is to give people the power to share and make the world more open and connected."* (and a quip here 7.27.12: *"And to make Mark Z. a pile of dough, having done little"*)

An Ethos grows around Purpose and is an intricate part of a goals strategy. The affect of Purpose can be measured, but as its object of focus moves slightly or massively, it finds a new life and possibly a new beginning. In that way, Purpose is the *"sighting system"* that guides the **Integrated Business Plan** (another chapter in this work) that seeks **Enduring Organization** (another chapter in this work) as a characteristic of The Great Workplace 2.0

"Touching the sky at ground level" is simply taking a lofty ideal and in practice, making it a visible, tangible daily event: On Purpose, with Purpose. Your Statement of Purpose should *"Connect, Engage and Collaborate"* with all Participants.

Your Purpose is the Fire in the center of your Tipi.

Values

Executive Summary:
- Values are those ideals and Principles (Codes of Conduct) that govern and influence **consistent actions and their corresponding results (Culture)** toward an organization's Purpose.
- Values are non-negotiable and need to be core to the Integrated Operating Plan.
- Values combined with the organization's Purpose (for the customer), and the Integrated Operating Plan, **ALIGN** all assets (Participants) of the organization to create **Enduring**.
- Defined and executed Values can and do make an organization **Remarkable**.

Values are in fact culturally bred and based, and influenced by Leadership. The Great Workplace 2.0 defines those Values pro-action and values guide decisions, conduct, and Innovation.

The difficulty in pro-defining most Core Values for entities is that these directives are subject to interpretation according to the personal values of a participant when there is NO overriding PURPOSE to the business at the beginning. It is difficult or impossible for an organization to define appropriate decision-making (values) when there is no defined reason (target) for being in business or customer-centric answer to, *"Why do we exist? When there is no defined Purpose, and loosely defined Values, most decisions will default to: "Make money/ Close the deal." "Make Money"* as an overt principle has proven itself to be wide-open to individual interpretation and is driven by a *"Value of the moment."*

Great Workplaces define the Purpose first, then define the process and principles involved in assuring that Purpose. The Core Values necessary to attain a consistent Purpose will be self-defined in this way.

Values are both supportive to the Purpose and defined by the Purpose.

Let's first take the Wikipedia definition of Values and see how they apply.

Value:

*"A **personal and cultural value** is a relative, ethic value, an assumption upon which implementation can be extrapolated. A value system is a set of consistent values and measures. A principle value is a foundation upon which other values and measures of integrity are based. Values are considered subjective, vary across people and cultures and are in many ways aligned with belief and belief systems. Types of values include ethical/moral values, doctrinal/ideological (religious, political) values, social values, and aesthetic values. It is debated whether some values are intrinsic."*

Note: "Values are considered subjective, vary across people and cultures and in many ways are aligned to belief systems…" And: "…an assumption upon which implementation can be extrapolated." In other words values can be and are employed as totally subjective…according to the viewer.

Then why is an organization's Values *"valuable"* or advantageous? They are in fact NOT of value at all…unless they are aligned with an overriding PURPOSE, and that PURPOSE is the ship's rudder. Further, Great Workplaces don't just talk Values; they live them, as does their Leadership.

In simple terms, Great Workplaces say: *"This is our ultimate reason for being in business for the customer (Purpose), and here is how (Values) we are going to prove it."*

Values then are a Discipline, a requirement for behavior. Values guide actions. As a dedicated athlete drives him or herself for achievement, so does The Great Workplace 2.0.

An aligned organization's Values create expectations of results. The organization's Culture defines the path to Purpose. Purpose defines the Values necessary to achieve Purpose. The *"Why"*, the *"How"* (Values and Differentiators) and the *"What"* (the product or service) are all in one big loop for success as defined by the Integrated Operating Plan.

Few if any organizations will actually say: *"We have NO values, no regard for concepts greater than ourselves and no regard for anything that can react to our actions (people)."* They will in fact discuss how they perceive they conduct business. They will in fact refer to their ideas that espouse what the leader or individual believes are in line with a corporate Mission. Or, they will respond with the platitude, *"Whatever it takes to get the Mission accomplished."* That might sound cool and aggressive, but it degenerates quickly to this: *"What are your Values?"* Answer: *"Whatever…"* (we'll wing it).

Here is an example of corporate values by one of the world's largest and most recognizable companies:

Boeing Corporate Values:
In all our relationships we will demonstrate our steadfast commitment to:

Leadership
- We will be a world-class leader in every aspect of our business: in developing every level of our team leadership skills, in our management performance, in the design, building and support of our products, and in our financial results.

Integrity
- We will always take the high road by practicing the highest ethical standards, and by honoring our commitments. We will take personal responsibility for our actions; treat everyone fairly, with trust and respect.

Quality
- We will strive for continuous quality improvement in all that we do, so that we will rank among the world's premier firms in customer, employee and community satisfaction.

Customer Satisfaction
- Satisfied customers are essential to our success. We will achieve total customer satisfaction by understanding what the customer wants and delivering it flawlessly.

People Working Together
- We recognize our strength and our competitive advantage is — and always will be — people. We will continually learn, and share ideas and knowledge. We will encourage cooperative efforts at every level and across all activities in our company.

A Diverse and Involved Team

- We value the skills, strengths and perspectives of our diverse team. We will foster a participatory workplace that enables people to get involved in making decisions about their work that advance our common business objectives.

Good Corporate Citizenship

- We will provide a safe workplace and protect the environment. We will promote the health and well-being of Boeing people and their families. We will work with our communities by volunteering and financially supporting education and other worthy causes.

Enhancing Shareholder Value

- Our business must produce a profit, and we must generate superior returns on the assets entrusted to us by our shareholders. We will ensure our success by satisfying our customers and increasing shareholder value.

In The Great Workplace, Core Values Do:

- Govern personal relationships
- Guide business processes
- Clarify who we are
- Articulate what we stand for
- Help explain why we do business the way we do
- Guide us on how to teach
- Inform us on how to reward
- Guide us in making decisions
- Underpin the whole organization
- Require no external justification
- Guide Visible, Tangible Leadership
- Require Transparency

In the Great Workplace, Core Values are Not:

- Operating *"practices"*. Practices are defined by Values and Purpose
- Business strategies. Strategies are directions to Purpose
- Cultural norms. *"Norms"* are an amalgam of individually selected practices
- Competencies. Skills are innate. Values are *"in-use"*
- Changed in response to market/ administration changes. Values are non-negotiable
- Used and interpreted individually. Values define the aligned actionable structure. They are supportive to the Purpose and defined by the Purpose.

Corporate Values are worthless if they are not Visible, not a part of the everyday *"Tribal Language."* If they are not taught, written, confirmed by acceptable actions then they are not a component of the Integrated Operating Plan.

If the Leadership of the organization does not Visibly and Tangibly support by actions AND speech, the Values of the organization, those Values become less than nothing to Participants (especially customers) the Values become a sarcastic joke. This in fact is the easiest and least controllable way to assure the demise of your organization and representative Leaders. Lose credibility and you lose your ability to positively influence people and direction.

Visible, Tangible leadership must remain credible. Credibility is, like Culture — *"Values in Action."* A respected leader cannot act in ways that discount the importance of Values. Put simply: Make a promise and keep it.

For Leaders who want to remain credible: If your organization is cutting costs, leave the Mercedes 500 S at home. If your organization espouses work ethic, be the first one in and the last to leave. If your organization Values honesty and Integrity, drop the after-hours girlfriend or boyfriend your wife or husband doesn't know about (but your employees probably do). BE the person the organization's Values dictate you to be.

Give your time to those who ask. Listen first, then respond to any question, honestly, even if the response is, *"I don't know, but will find out."* When having conversations, stand square shouldered to the person, and look them in the eyes. Standing sideways is deflection and looking anywhere but at that person shows a lack of true interest.

Examples of Failure: This is fairly easy. Ask ANY person in any organization what the organizational Values are. If they cannot answer or have only a vague recollection from some time ago, the organization has no REAL Values. Unfortunately, MOST cannot answer that question, except in Great Workplaces. If someone *"kinda"* knows and makes a decent attempt at sentences that are based in SOME defined value, it is time to re-train and adjust the Tribal Language. This also shows that if your values are too complex, too philosophical to recall, the organization needs to rewrite them, not change them.

How to Discover or Rediscover Values:

It took my own company over two months to redefine and agree to our Values. We discussed the obvious choices: Integrity, Honesty, Hard Work, Customer Satisfaction, and so on. And ALL those remained as core reasoning in our chosen Values. But we chose Values that go beyond the easy option of copying someone else's named Values.

Champion's are:
1) Second Best Isn't Good Enough™. In effort or action for any participant to our success.
2) The Right People Doing the Right Things, Right®. This defines our own staff and our choice of staff for our clients.

3) TEAMWORK & Collaboration. Champion has multiple offices that need to work together for our Purposes (Make Staffing Easy. A Better Job, A Better Life for our candidates and associates).

Without explaining in great detail what components go into each Value, these Values make total and complete sense to our Staff. We talk about them every day. They are in writing. We live them. They are non-negotiable. They are public. They are part of our internal performance review system, because they are Culture-based, directive to our Purpose(s) and the Path to achieving our Purpose(s). Our Purpose(s) in turn, define these values. And Champion is expanding. Our previous Values were NOT discarded. They were rolled up into new phrasing that made the Values Actionable Today.

A side note: If *"Second Best Isn't Good Enough"* is one of our Values and as the Leader (Chief) at Champion, does that mean I should buy a 600 S Benz? No. Values are not *"things."* Besides, I do have the best vehicle: a Prius. It reflects my heritage values (Be gentle on Mother Earth and be thinking about the Seventh Generation into the future).

How you can discover and make Values critical to your organization? Yep, thus is the $64,000 question:

1) Start with your Purpose for doing what you do beyond making money. If that is still unanswered, go to the Chapter on Purpose, first.

2) When you THOROUGHLY understand (or have adjusted) your Purpose, write it out beyond one word or sentence. Talk about the *"Why"* of your purpose. Write out the paths to achieving that Purpose (for your customer) in DETAIL. Answer the question: *"Why would your potential customer believe that Purpose to be important to them?"*

3) Define and understand the *"How"* of your product or service (Differentiators). *"How"* are your differentiators from the industry *"Norm"* (The "What")

4) Now define the actionable disciplines of behaviors and attitudes that will best define your path to achieving, in a repeatable fashion, your Ultimate Purpose for your Customer. Are those disciplines realistic? Are they demonstrable (actions that can be measured)? Are those behaviors and paths able to be translated into "Values" that will be non-negotiable and meaningful internally and externally?

5) Present your findings to trusted business associates, board members, coaches and family members for feedback. If you are re-defining or are in the first stages of creating Values in an existing organization, talk to trusted associates, internally and externally. Call your legal counsel, accounting firm partners, banking relations. Know the platform on which these people stand. Take their advice knowing they are not you, and will not be ultimately accountable for your decision. Or just call me.

Values: The path to your Purpose. Disciplines. The foundation for deliverables that are non-negotiable. Values in action can make an Organization Remarkable.

Why, What, How:
Products and Services

Executive Summary:

- You KNOW the What. The What of your products or services is the base feature-set of your offerings, what everyone else offers, that makes your product or service a commodity.

- The Why is your Purpose for the customer, the reason you went into business above and beyond money: Your Purpose becomes your customer's Purpose in buying from you because it includes you, your company, your people, your values and your actions. The Customer decides to digest it, or move it on to THEIR customer.

- The How is what truly differentiates your actual product, your organization and your team from competitors.

Most organizations have the What firmly in place and stop there. The Great Workplace organizations use their Purpose (Why) to fuel their How, and emerge as leaders in their field. In that way, good organizations can become Remarkable. Read on, it gets easier....

In his book, Start with Why: How Great Leaders Inspire Everyone To Take Action, Simon Sinek makes the case that Leaders who focus on Why the organization exists in the first place will always win. In each organization, most people in authority know the *"What"* (*"We make screw machine parts." "We're a billings and collections service."*). That part's easy. Customers who perceive that your product or service falls into the commodity category will tell you: *"You all produce the same thing, so let's talk price, delivery and extended terms."* The customer just told you that your offering or your explanation of your offering lacks Purpose, or worse, lacks commitment to THEIR Purpose or their NEED (to achieve THEIR Purpose).

And yes, in today's globally competitive economy, it seems tougher to make a better mousetrap. Costs and price pressures and purchasing agents simply seem to ignore the differentiators and go immediately to pricing as the only significant differentiator. And the rules of this game seem to change as you breathe. Couple that with buyers today making YOU feel like the commodity, and they seem to do that with increasing pleasure, especially with the buyer whom you are certain is talking down to you, and not listening.

That is a tough pill to swallow for an entrepreneur or business executive that has designed or approved the product or service being offered. Someone just told you they don't see the same value in YOUR offering that YOU do. It hurts. It makes you indignant.

Remarkable Organizations, The Great Workplaces, understand the commodity *"bitter pill"* and focus on their original reasons for being in business: the WHY. The WHY extends to their product or service, and is indistinguishable from it. Why is for the customer.

What The Great Workplace organizations offer that make them Remarkable:

1) The founder/CEO understands that he/she can no longer Innovate products or services solely on their own. There was only one Thomas Edison and even he had a legion of assistants (his Muckers, as he called them). Eventually, your immediate brilliant ideas run out, and so does the patience of your entire *"Participants"* base. Humbling, but true.

2) The Great Workplace Leaders create, discover and make a daily sermon from the organization's Purpose. True leaders make the Purpose Crystal Clear, in their own minds and the minds of their Participants. Clarity of Purpose — they live it, and develop others to live it.

3) The Great Workplace Leaders insist that the organization's Values (that support Purpose) are topics of conversations, and they Visibly, Tangibly support those values as the foundation for delivering the Purpose to all participants.

4) The Great Workplace Leaders have chosen the Right People who share Purpose and Values, and they spend time developing those people to lead the charge.

5) The Great Workplace practices Collaboration, at every opportunity, in developing products or services that will become Remarkable. They KNOW that Innovation and improvements can come from anywhere and from anyone if asked, including outsiders, but especially the Customer. Leaders Engage participants to Innovate, create the environment for logic (creative and deductive problem-solving) AND serendipity (unplanned

discovery) and focus on the future, to create the Enduring Organization.

6) The organization's Operating Plan is Aligned with Innovation, Collaboration, Values, Purpose, and the Right People supporting these characteristics.

Remarkable organizations have a crystal-clear understanding of their Why (Purpose) and it permeates everything they do, and HOW they do it. The Purpose is their engine for Innovation, Creativity and Persistence (One of the four *"P's"* of Leadership: Purpose, Persistence, Principles and Passion). Like a trained Special Forces warrior, they simply will never quit. It is not a job, it is their calling.

The *"Magic"* in Remarkable organizations' ability to produce products and services that outsell their competition, or are considered "leaders" in their field, comes from knowing that a product or service is not bought alone, but that astute buyers are buying the product/service, the organization, the values of the organization in delivering those products and service, the people who make or create the product or service and the Purpose with which it is delivered. By utilizing every resource available, they are able to stay not only one-step ahead in the field, but also one-step ahead of their customers.

Integrated Operating Plan

Executive Summary:

- Yes, to many, this is THE dreaded part of business success. There are startup plans, banking or finance plans, marketing plans, product plans and plans to handle Holiday parties. So, many owners or CEOs simply don't do it, or give it a half-hearted effort, and go back to working IN, not ON the business.

- The Great Workplaces of today and the future know that without a true Integrated Operating Plan, they will be tossed about by the frustrations of not only economic change, but everyday business.

- The Integrated Operating Plan functions as the poles of your Tip. It aligns your organization with its Purpose.

Owners and CEOs of organizations had or have a Vision for their ventures. It runs constantly in their minds like the best Blu-ray video they have ever seen. Scenes change, with new characters and new outcomes appearing, which keeps the Vision exciting. Fanfare and awards banquets fill the end-game. It produces Passion, hopes, wishes and dreams.

The problem is that Hopes, Wishes and Dreams are NOT sustainable strategic plans. They will however, produce the *"What"* of the business (the product, service), perhaps the *"Why"* (Purpose for the customer, Vision, Mission), but never the *"How"* (differentiating processes).

Live with it my friend, and get on to creating a walk-able path to your future. The Integrated Operating Plan is your 3-D Navigable Map to your success, your future, your Purpose realized, and your Goals and Objectives. Devised properly, it will have voice-directions, cautions and route recalculations, alternative routes built-in and Threat notifications. But it also has a non-negotiable core that keep your Tipi secure and on a solid footing.

Envision the poles in your organization's Tipi to be the operating plans for every facet of your business: manufacturing, product/ service design, distribution, finance and more (or less) depending upon the complexity of your business. You or several of your *"Right People"* have laid those plans out to encompass the directions, assets, objectives, continual improvements, threats that your best minds can see for today and the future.

The numbers look good, your assumptions are conservative and logical, and overall each plan seems to be within your grasp. Consensus has been built within each functional area. Your roadmap is laid out. Don't put it in that desk drawer just yet. And don't publish it for your staff.

Remarkable organizations have you beat already. They too have solid plans, well-thought through by passionate and talented people. But they centered their plans into and on their Purpose, Values, and Culture (Values in Action). They integrated the requirements of Visible Tangible Leadership, with Tools and Transparent Integrity. Remarkable organizations not only show the path, but The Why and The How they will approach their plan.

Remarkable organizations use the collar at the top of their Tipi (where the poles meet) to create a foundation that will Endure. It is where all unit plans integrate into one. The plans are aligned with the organization's Purpose(s) and Values.

Purpose, Values, Culture (*Values In Action*) and Leadership drive the success of the organization. These are the behaviors that overcome obstacles, the Values that drive great decisions, and the Purpose(s) that are the beacons at the end of the path.

Remarkable organizations remind themselves of the Why (Purpose) at every turn, for every action, and especially for times of confusion. The Customer is the Purpose and the Values are the How.

Your Values and Purpose (Why) are non-negotiable (they can be tweaked along the way) and because of that, need to be an integral part of your How (uniqueness, separation from competitors, Innovation) you will succeed.

Sun Tzu wrote: *"The consummate Leader cultivates the moral law [Values in Action, and Purpose] and strictly adheres to method [plan] and discipline [again, values in action]; thus it is in his power to control success."* The Leadership and Plan function upon Values, Purpose and Culture (*Values In Action*).

Leaders formulate the detailed plan, infuse it with reminders of Why and How, communicate the plan with Passion, Vision, and supply the roadmap to success at every opportunity.

The plan is Enduring and set on success. Again, Sun Tzu; *"In respect of military method [How], we have, firstly, Measurement; secondly, Estimation of quantity; thirdly, Calculation; fourthly, Balancing of chances; fifthly, Victory."* Sun Tzu sounds like he attended Case Western

University's Weatherhead School of Management, then went on to achieve a Weatherhead 100 Fastest Growing Privately Held business award (my own company has multiple Weatherhead 100 Awards).

The Integrated Operating Plan balances the What, the Why and the How. It integrates the foundation of an organization with strategies (How) based upon the Purpose(s) and the Why.

Here is the Secret Sauce practiced by Remarkable Organizations:

- Each organization has planned the objectives and the paths for each "Unit" within the organization: Manufacturing, Purchasing/ Supply Chain, Financial, Customer Service and so on. Smaller organizations plan each function, even when ALL those functions are confined within a smaller group of people, accomplishing multiple functions.

- Some plans are incredibly detailed with charts, graphs, matrices, and contingency charts. Some plans are simple, one- to two-page documents of guidance and intents.

- ALL effective Unit plans begin with or are infused with the organization's overall Purpose, as it relates to the end customer. Each unit plan shows the objective of Purpose that motivates and guides actions, intents, contingency plans and "opportunity plans." Values are quoted in action plans or those actions steps are infused with the language of those values.

- Each plan reminds itself of the Why of the business. Achieving Purpose is the thread that connects all actions in a Unit plan.

But no Unit plan stands alone. It Connects, Engages, and Collaborates with other Unit plans, and the Integrated Operating Plan itself. And there is the simple secret: Connect with other

Unit plans, Engage with their objectives and plans to discover efficiencies and overlaps, Collaborate assets and objectives around the Purpose of the organization, with the Customer in focus. Collaboration and Teamwork align the powers of the organization to achieve objectives, not to be contentious. The functional TEAM is the organization as a whole, not the just the individual Units. With Purpose as the end-game, the How becomes engaged with the Why.

Then, the Integrated Operating Plan is born from the Collaboration of each unit plan, into a single, aligned method (Organizational) of assuring the Purpose is met and goals are achieved.

It sounds complex and simple all at the same time, and yes, it is. To be an effective document, it needs to be nurtured and massaged, lengthened and then edited to a readable, digestible in one sitting, document.

Passionate, visionary, owners and managers know that this is working ON, not IN the business itself. They create, with their Right People, the map for the future.

The Integrated Operating Plan is rich with narrative that tells not only the organization's story (History, Victories, People, blockades that have been demolished, mistakes from which learning and growth have been born, and The Vision of the Future), but the accountabilities of all Participants (and Units) in the ultimate delivery of the Purpose.

It is used to Align all units to the central themes of the Why.

The Integrated Operating Plan will immerse all Participants, New Employees, Vendors and Community in the Vision, Values and Purpose of the organization. It is used when the

Right People are promoted to new positions of accountability. It reminds these Right People of the Vision and the Path. Unit plans are used to educate and direct participants in the How of their roles and to know where Collaboration and Teamwork need to be deployed. Owners and Managers refer to the core of this document when reminding Participants of the Why to what they are working on or in.

Remarkable organizations work ON their business. They work on their Path to Purpose. And being BIG is not a component of Remarkable.

The Final Bonus Step: The one-page summation document

Through the process of discovering how and why organizations achieve becoming remarkable, I kept running into owners who referred to their *"One-Page Plan."* Not having one myself, I didn't really *"get it"* until a close friend told me to wake up and Read Verne Harnish's book, *Mastering the Rockefeller Habits*. He also gave me a list of people he knew who ran their business using the book and the one-page plan as their core *"field manual."* I had already talked with most of them.

Three-hours later, I *"stole"* the book from my friend's office and devoured it. Overnight. Yes, I'm serious.

Then I started to backtrack with Remarkable Organization owners and many whom I had yet to meet with. The question was simple: *"Tell me about your one-pager?"* Their answers were simple and boiled down to: *"Yes we have one; we use it to measure how we are doing according to our Plan. It summarizes our progress, but always begins with our Mission or Purpose."*

Yes, they all had *"Unit"* plans, Culture Stories and Integrated Operating plans at some level of complexity and depth.

They all had a one-page strategic plan or a close version of it. Some even had it in their suit pocket, in their portfolio or on their mobile device. It simply summarizes the critical measurables that confirm the ultimate Purpose and Vision.

Remarkable organizations have unit plans that speak to the ultimate purpose of the organization. These Unit plans show the Collaborative alignment needed with other Unit plans and the Integrated Operating plan. The result is that all their poles in the Tipi converge to the Integrated Operating Plan itself.

And the Most Remarkable organizations and Leaders have a one page, measureable *"Cheat Sheet"* or *"score card"* that tells them how they are doing.

Examples of failure:

In most cases of failure from organizations analyzed for this work, it is not outright closure of the business that is the sad story. It is the unrealized potential or stagnation of progress (in some cases this lead to closure). The Vision was lost to daily struggles. The Purpose became far less important than a Mission (short term) or the Purpose was diluted to a restatement of an organization-centric goal (Intrinsic, *"Be the leader in ..."* type statements):

The manufacturing organization where the generation #3 leader pulled so far away from the Vision of the Founder that the company literally became a place to *"play"* CEO, not to make a difference. He retreated to his wealth (inherited) and avoided making plans that could right the ship. The organization's Values were forgotten and its Culture became void. The CEO didn't work hard, so then no one else cared ... because there was no evident plan, no evident culture. People worked for their paychecks, push the lever, pull the lever, not for the organization.

A real, integrated plan that refocused efforts on the Values of the company and the Purpose for their customers, along with future product plans could have put them back into competition. A separate division of the company, guided by its own Values and Purpose, and Right People, was and is highly successful … under new ownership and leadership.

The 60+ year-old, profitable manufacturer wanted to reduce incredibly high turnover. They talked about correcting the Culture by implementing Values and Purpose beyond their ISO quality statements. The company is still doing an okay business, but turnover remains one of the highest in the area. How they do what they do is solid. But no one internally knows it. Not having Values and Culture as core principles for how they do what they do is keeping the organization from reaching its true potential.

Example of Successes:

A startup online marketing firm has grown from two to more than 30 people in six years. The owner knew exactly what niche he wanted to serve, made non-negotiable operating plans to do so, and cemented the Values, Purpose and therefore Culture early on. They have turned down business where their Values and Purpose did not fit, even when they could have hired an extra person to execute the new direction. Holding firm to their Integrated Plan has led them to success. How do I know? They turned down Champion as a customer, and told me why. We went, successfully, with another successful Great Workplace.

A producer of Database systems took off like a rocket, about 5 years into business. Most work is custom, but built upon an original backbone. Their growth has exceeded 1,000 percent over and over and they have *"graduated"* from Enduring to *"Rock Star"* status. They know their "What" (Database applications) but stress that their *"How"* (uniqueness) comes from their Values and Purpose(s) not only for each customer but for their own people, community, vendors and influencers. Their Operating Plan has Integrated the numbers and their market strategy firmly with the published and communicated Values and Purpose. Each individual joining the firm is immersed with the Values BEFORE their first interview and in the planned full life cycle (hire to retire) immersion process. It goes hand-in-hand with job objectives, duties and Tools. The Operating Plan inspires enthusiastic performance and retention.

The leading producer of a simple, yet technical product has stayed a leader in their field by a constant reflection on, *"Are we achieving our Customer's ultimate Purpose? Are we staying true to our Values?"* These are integrated into all product, manufacturing and distribution plans, right down to manufacturing machine maintenance. It is the core of their supply chain, Human Resources, finance and Internal promotions/ succession planning. It is the core of business-decision processes. Focusing on the How and Why reduces "distractions" for all involved in their success.

I would not be so presumptuous to tell you how to plan YOUR business. That is your Vision, and your Vision should define the mechanics. Your advisors and Board will help.

To be truly remarkable, to be a truly Great Workplace, your plans must integrate your Values and Purpose, not as a preamble to any plan, but as the "How" to be successful, and Enduring. Remember that markets and short-term strategies may change markedly, but your Values and Purpose(s) will be the foundation that allows you the flexibility, and, the footing to change without fear.

The poles in your Tipi must all meet at the collar if it is to hold up. And your collar, Values and Purpose (The WHY) secure it together.

The Right People
Doing the Right Things, Right ®

Executive Summary:
- Organizations that are able to hire or contract (including Vendors) the Right People to do the Right Things Right, do this on and with Purpose.
- This is accomplished with an objective system that focuses on finding people to achieve performance objectives, not just fill a chair. Many companies attempt this with fleeting results.
- The Great Workplace 2.0 uses a secret sauce that you don't: *"Connect: Engage: Collaborate"* internally and externally.

The Great Workplaces BUILD a great and remarkable organization by systematically hiring the Right People. They guide them to do the Right Things, and to do those things, Right. The Great Workplaces immerse the Right People in their purpose, goals and culture. They show them the path towards goals. They teach them the organization's values. They are taught the Purpose of the work that is being done within the Purpose of the organization. And ... they do this EARLY in the process. They Connect with people, they Engage these people, and they Collaborate within and outside their organization with all *"participants to their success."*

The Right People are motivated to follow the journey because they identify personally with and are engaged with the organization's values. Remarkable Organizations ask these people, *"In what ways are you going to contribute to our and your successes?"* As opposed to *"Can You?"* Remarkable Organizations focus on developing skills for their environment (advancing knowledge and performance capabilities). Great Workplace organizations both lead and follow their Right people … and get out of their way. This operating Purpose extends to Vendors, Board, Contracted assets and community.

The Great Workplaces have developed a methodology of hiring the Right People, direct them to do the Right things, and nurture them to do those things, Right. These Remarkable Organizations have recognized that Great Talent is different than *"resume experience"* and have taken the time to structure how to identify and match the Right person with the Right assignment. They have spent the time to develop the Right environment for the Right people. And, they hold these people accountable for results, both in spirit and in performance reviews.

Struggling workplaces have created and saddled themselves with irritating and costly turnover, ill-suited but convenient management, and few if any reasons for good people to want to do things right.

"Accountability" for Participants takes the form of management ignoring the good results, and grinding on mistakes. In Great Workplaces, the owner/founder/CEO has taken the step to not only put structure to performance reviews, but inserted hiring methodology as the first step to Greatness. Great Workplace owners and managers have *"let go"* of the desire to decide good or bad performance according to their *"mood of the day"*. Being emotionally attached to every event, especially aberrations of behavior from employees is not only typical for small to medium-sized business owners, but is both our strength and weakness.

The Great Workplace chiefs have simply taken another step up the long ladder to applicable leadership.

A recent Global Workforce Study (Towers Watson®, a global performance consulting organization) shows that 63 percent of U.S. workers are not fully engaged in their work. Of that, 27 percent lacked the energy and enablement to engage consistently, 13 percent are not willing to engage, and 23 percent are completely disengaged. Just 37 percent of workers were found to be consistently highly engaged in their work.

The lack of engagement is most companies will result in higher than normal employee turnover, and that can result in a constant battle for endurance of the organization.

To give a first-person *"results of engagement"* outcome: One of the TOP Great Workplaces in NE Ohio emphasizes a thorough understanding of the organization's Purpose for the customer, taking away employee distractions, an ongoing Immersion into their entire operations, creating a true Succession Plan for the Top Executives that creates the *"1,000 years"* (my quote) culture: This manufacturing organization has less than 6 percent turnover, and most of that is on company terms. Voluntary Turnover is about 2 percent. This compares to studies of all industries including the low turnover rates in high-tech and government where Voluntary Turnover averages 15 percent (SHRM study 2010-2011 Database Bench Marking)

Further, according to a 2008 SHRM (Society for Human Resource Management) study, the cost to replace and hire new staff may be as high as 60 percent of an employee's annual salary, whereas total costs of replacement, including training and loss of productivity, can range from 90 percent to 200 percent of an employee's annual salary. Those expenditures can be difficult to absorb, whether an organization is a small company or a large global firm.

Granted, a certain percentage of workers today will NOT engage in their work, ever. It makes one wonder though, why organizations have those workers around long enough to be counted as "Workers". When The Great Workplaces of today find that "will not engage" person, they disappear quickly and quietly. In The Great Workplace, those people stand out like dull squares surrounded by sparkling marbles.

The Great Workplaces save money, add to their bottom line, and create a better Culture by reducing turnover through more systematic hiring and engagement of their Participants.

The secret sauce that permeates the environment:

"Connect : Engage : Collaborate ©"

The core of Connect: Engage: Collaborate is Purposeful Conversations. These conversations are based in respect, common courtesy, and an openness typically reserved for private discussions. There is no "hidden code" or innuendo involved. There is no hidden agenda. This is not only a component of the work culture, but a powerful component of insightful hiring methodology.

Engagement is critical to the success of The Great Workplace. It defines both attitude toward and perception of the work's Purpose, and the ability to connect with the work. I will go a step further, from a hands-on perspective: A great talent in a Purpose-lacking or negative environment will achieve the same below-expectations work as someone who is only half as talented, but engaged. The great talent, not engaged, is an easy recruit to another organization.

Notice the lack of engagement you may experience on the shop floor, or coding of software, or processing of invoices: do you really want someone who doesn't care about being excellent to make a product for your customer or a person who is not thinking about the customer experience to calculate special invoices and send them out? Open your eyes. It happens all the time, but less in The Great Workplaces.

Then there is the elusive topic of Retention. Great Workplaces have the ability to retain high to good performers in Remarkable fashion due to having a structure to hiring, public display of Purpose, Visible Tangible leadership, and performance reviews/ incentives. Their approach is holistic and considers the Participant (employee) throughout the entire work-lifespan of that participant ("hire to retire", so to speak).

The Great Workplaces give their people reasons to want to do good work. People are not treated like commodities. People can feel and sense that they have value, beyond their payroll number. Their objectives are as important to them as they are to you.

Hiring the Right Person is not an easy task. Conventional methods of hiring have not only permeated most companies today as a legacy, but have been ignored by the people most able to change them: *"C"* level executives, and Human Resource *"executives"*.

Most small- to medium-size organization CEOs *"recognize"* talent, but delegate finding that talent to the HR department who might have little or no training in best practices to do so. To be fair to HR professionals, the majority of their responsibilities are in Compliance activities (workers' compensation, benefits, EEO, legal, reporting) and evaluation/hiring can be a new concept, in part due to their lack of operations or management experience.

Great Workplaces will support their talents and expertise, in a structured hiring methodology, where they can and do excel. Their stumbling block is in the ad-hoc and legacy hiring processes already existing in an organization. Many astute HR practitioners are actively involved in their professional associations, and take great pleasure in devouring the newest best practices shared at seminars, and development sessions they attend in and outside of work hours. They return to work with proven ideas, only to be met with the brick walls of legacy practices.

For CEOs of potential Great Workplaces; listen to HR professionals who have taken the time to understand solid hiring systems. Get them involved with the workforce they will service. Give them a thorough, hands-on immersion into what that workforce actually does and who does it best, and why. Get them out of their offices! Hint: one of the major reasons *"operations"* people don't have a high regard for HR is their lack of actual hands-on operations experience or exposure. Most HR folks don't wear a work shirt with their name on it. Astute organizations will help develop impactful HR professionals by giving them development opportunities in the guts of their organizations. Yes, some of the TOP HR professionals I have met actually get (or have insisted on receiving) hands-on training in what the workers do in their organization. It is well-known that Lincoln Electric, Cleveland (not a company in our research, too big, public) required ALL white-collar employees to spend six months on the shop floor making their products before beginning their career functions. This gets them engaged with the work, the people and the culture.

Great Workplaces do not confuse hiring The Right People to do the Right Things, Right, with *"Finding TOP Talent"* (A newer Human Resources term). And for the most part Managers of Remarkable Organizations consider the concept of *"TOP Talent*

Acquisition" a result of having built the foundation of a remarkable organization, not a fancy substitute for *"Hiring Right."* Top Talent is a term best used as a category of exceptional people, not as a term to be sought after. *"The Right Person"* describes a comparison of a defined profile to the single opportunity.

The Great Workplaces of today create a system of hiring The Right People based upon the belief that there is a "Right Person" for every function:

Here is the secret sauce The Great Workplaces put into play: Knowledgeable and accountable line managers first define the function to be filled in terms of goals (performance goals or objectives) to be achieved by an incumbent. They analyze job functions into realistic and definable separate components. They ask questions like: what exactly will this person (or function, from an objective standpoint) actually do on a daily basis? Too often, hiring Managers (and Human Resource people) treat a job as though it were one single, amalgamated function, and this will confuse the ability to later analyze the necessary skills, talents and previous performances of the desired candidate.

The function is then analyzed for the skills it will take to achieve acceptable (and above) levels of performance. The Great Workplace is highly objective in this. This includes an analysis of current best performers, the skills and values they brought to the organization when hired and their path of development in achieving success to date. Great Workplaces know that great performers are not simply acquired, they are lead and developed.

"Skills" needed are then extrapolated into *"Performance Based Experiences"* (Achievements and how these have been achieved. Can this be duplicated or extrapolated into our opportunity?), best defined as past achievements, with an eye on the skills needed being a realistic result of those defined experiences. The

smartest hiring authorities do not confuse defined skills with perceived experience or assumed skills from that experience.

Add to this the short- and long-term goals (performance objectives) needed to be achieved in this function, then redefine the skills necessary to achieve BOTH the functional necessities AND the goals (they may NOT be the same, but won't be exclusionary). Goals are defined in terms of metrics, outcomes and needed growth potential achieved by the incumbent (in today's business world, succession-planning is highly relevant).

Points of interaction (Teamwork, Collaboration) are defined and with that the skills and attitudes relative to achieving productive relationships are outlined. Style, values, communication skills are defined in relation to organizational values, existing culture (*Values In Action*) and methods of interaction (one on one, distance collaboration, subordinate/superior, outside customers/ inside customers).

Organizational *"Values"* are then put into *"people identifiers"*: What values do we need to have already in place with an individual, and what values or components of values can we develop in good people? How to recognize the presence of these core values in the interviewing process are defined, written and agreed to by all parties involved … relative to the function or objectives. Will this person be able to identify with our core values? How will we know?

Then, and only then, is the *"Profile To Be Hired"* put together for the search. But the true differentiator between the most effective hiring methodologies and "also-ran" attempts is that The Great Workplaces define WHY that specific profile would want to work at their company, in that function, from the point of view of the person being recruited, and the relative availability in the marketplace of the profile to be hired. It is never answered by:

"We're a good company, with good benefits, competitive salaries and people like it here."

The *"attraction factor"* takes a deeper dive than a coffee conversation between HR and a hiring authority, and we'll get into that at the end of this chapter. Let me review the process:

- Define the measurable objectives of the function.

- Define the discoverable skills, talents and abilities to accomplish the objectives. Do NOT define these in terms of *"years of experience doing the same functions at another company"*. That is the hit and miss methodology of Legacy hiring. It does not work well.

- Discuss the findings and have all in the hiring process agree to objective standards of measurement. This includes target Values (Work values) and items like *"work approach"*, management style, collaborative skills, teamwork skills, communication style, ability to step up in greater responsibility, should all be included. Caution: "styles" and personal items other than values should be without doubt, set to an objective standard that reflects the actual job function. It is plain silly to include *"exceptional communication and team-building skills"* in a profile for a person who will work alone.

- Discuss in a creative way, where and how these standards can be found in a candidate's experience. Define levels of previous performances that will fit, in achievements that are similar in nature to what you have defined as objectives to be accomplished.

- Define the challenges for the person tackling this assignment. *"Challenges"* are what will attract the Right Person. You are looking for a person to improve something are you not? Then again, if what you need is a person to MAINTAIN a set of functions, perhaps looking for a person who wants to improve their function and career will be over-hiring. The realistic question here is: If you want a true top performer to handle this function, at what time-frame are you willing and able to lose this person?

- Finally, define, from the candidate's point of view, why this entire opportunity would interest this person.

There is a key factor that The Great Workplaces really *"get"* in hiring the Right People: The Right Person does NOT get excited about doing the same thing for the next five years that he/she has done for the last 10 years, with no growth, no new challenges, and no new horizon. The only reason a good person will have to accept that same opportunity is to make (or demand) more money, while they are looking for a bigger challenge.

An example: As a Recruiter, I was meeting with a top HR person in a solid company. This person had just defined (demanded) a profile for a search where the person the organization was seeking was directly experienced from their industry, "must have" 10 years minimum experience (in all aspects of the job) and would have little or no potential to move up. The salary being offered was "average". Asked WHY this person doing the same job at a competitor would want to move to my client, the HR person basically said "we're a good company, and treat our people well". I was underwhelmed.

I took a facility tour with the General Manager, met a few operations people and got a good *"feel"* for the culture. Meeting back with the HR person I took an opportunity to *"teach"* this person about hiring top people: First, I knew what this HR person did for their company, their work history and some achievements, and could guess what they were earning. I then said: "I'm looking for an HR person for another client, let me run this past you (I

NEVER however actually recruit from a client)… and proceeded to tell the HR person about the job, EXACTLY what this HR person was doing now. Same size company, same duties, same potential, and same salary. I then asked who they could recommend for the position, but ended with *"What about you?"*

Their response was anticipated:
"I would NOT be interested at all."

"Why?"

"It sounds like exactly what I am doing here, same potential and same money. I might be interested IF it had bigger challenges, better potential, and of course, more money."

My response was strategic: *"What I just described to you was actually YOUR job now, and you would not be interested. If you are not interested in moving laterally, why do you think the person YOU want to hire for your company, laterally, would be recruitable for your company?"*

He stopped in his tracks and for about 15 seconds and said nothing. Thankfully, his reaction was to laugh and say: *"You got me Schepens, and I get it. Let's talk about the person we want to hire, again."*

Hiring with and on purpose may sound *"Normal"* to many organizations, difficult, but normal. And to those organizations, we say: You are on the way or are already there!

In defining the characteristics of The Great Workplace 2.0, we met with organizations that are not now, nor ever will be a Great Workplace, until certain habits are changed, with Purpose.

The most striking deficits inherent in struggling workplaces is in their methodology of seeking and hiring new employees: it is sloppy, revolves around taking poorly written job descriptions and in the stroke of a pen, turning that job description into a profile containing multiple *"Must Have's"* (essentially, 'must have' done this exact job elsewhere, preferably at a competitor, and be able to "hit the ground running" at our place).

That job description is then converted into an ad, or listing on the organization's hard-to-find *"careers"* section of their website, where it sits forever, lacking any attention. Top talent (the ones who should be hired) see all the *"must have's"* and boring job-duty descriptions, and move away from the site. Unfortunately, the ones who do apply have been unemployed since their last stint at a fast-food drive-thru 18 months ago.

Job descriptions that are converted to *"Must have"* resume descriptions do NOT Connect much less *"Engage"* with the Right People. Those people are turned off.

In the description of the *"profile to be hired"* There is no analysis of actual skills needed to be successful, no analysis of the functions to be accomplished or goals to be met. Most Non-Great Workplaces figure that if the person has *"10-years experience"* in what the hiring company does, then they should know WHAT to do. First, that is a very false assumption, and most importantly, a description written that way will be of no interest to a person gainfully employed who is seeking a *"better opportunity"*.

So the (not Great Workplace) hiring organization focuses on reading resumes that have identifiable buzzwords in them, an appropriate amount of experience (5, 10, 15 years) and an acceptable tenure to positions (without asking why regarding job changes).

If the position(s) to be filled are in the high-turnover arena, they do little or no analysis of the reasons behind the turnover and therefore have no true plans how to correct the flow, even though it will be costing them big money, customers and their best people (exiting) all at the same time.

Compared to the hiring methodologies in Great Workplaces, the non-great workplace methodology looks like (is this yours?):

1) The line manager identifies an open position and seeks out the Human Resource department. To the operations person, HR are the ones who keep and approve headcount and are the ones management has said everything "has to go through". Typically, line managers are not allowed to seek new hires on their own, in large part due to company policies, EEO, and protocol. They look at hiring through HR to be a pain in the neck.

2) The line manager tells HR "I need an engineer". Or more accurately a "Product Engineer". After the requisite "why do you NEED this person and how much experience do you need?" discussion, the HR person looks in the book of job descriptions (not updated within the last many years) and pulls out the correct one. A copy is made, given to the line manager: "Are those requirements in line?"

3) Salary is discussed: "I'd like to keep the pay within the budget. So let's say $40-$50K." The budget will allow $58K to start, more with the CEO approval. The idea to look low without defining excellence being needed is in reaction to the individual's needs to look like they are saving the company money.

4) HR responds by saying that an ad for the internet (the job description is repeated in the ad, with "10 years of similar experience required in our product lines" added, and "Only those qualified need apply" thrown in as a time-saver for HR) will be written and that qualified resumes will be forwarded to the line manager for review. HR also says, "If I can't find anyone in a couple weeks for this, I'll fax it to 6 or 7 "agencies" to see if

they have anyone on file." It is preceded by "I'll have to try on my own for awhile, that is why the company hired me. If we get into trouble, I'll use an 'agency'." When the recruiting service is eventually called, the maximum information the HR person will impart is equivalent to: "We need a Product Engineer with 10 years of Hydraulics experience. If you have anyone, email the resume to me so I can see if we already have it from our ads. If we are interested in your person, I will email you back. We won't pay more than X% fee and we take 120 days to pay. I need a one-year guarantee." Hardly highly informative and Motivating.

5) And the games begin. This is where knowledgeable hiring professionals say *"Hope, Wishes and Dreams are NOT strategic plans."*

Does this sound like you? Hiring The Right People to do The Right Things, Right ... is part of the Integrated Operating Plan. And as such, it is a method, a structure, which never changes. The plan to "Acquire" the right talent is defined, refined and is a part of organizational values. After all, if certain customer goals are to be met, and there is little control over the functions and the people in them that deliver that value, how can the value to the customer be certain?

Circling back to the profile-to-be-hired stage with a Great Workplace: The hiring manager's discussion with HR is NOT brief, and may involve the collaboration of many people including the CEO, and not surprisingly, an outside third party.

Great Workplaces, almost to a fault, realize that recruiting, hiring, developing and retaining an effective workforce that will support the organization's vision(s) and Purpose, begins with strategic hiring.

They also acutely recognize that the Right Person needs to match the function and its future and that the organization needs to build the core *"Right People"* incrementally. The *"Right"* person for a certain function may NOT necessitate finding a *"top 5 percent"* talent. Or, the organization, function and future for that person may NOT be able to attract that *"Top 5 percent"* talent. Perhaps today, the BEST an organization can do is to hire a competent individual to handle the tasks at hand to achieve a 10 percent increase toward a goal or in efficiency/ output or effectiveness.

Perhaps the organization has yet to be able to attract a person who can *"Hit the ground running"* and take off from there. A Great Workplace takes one for the team, hires a person who has the desire to become a 5 percent-er, and develops that person from there.

But what Great Workplaces that are building themselves do NOT do is hire someone who cannot relate to the organization's values, purpose, visions and culture (Values in Action). But first, The Great Workplace (of the future) knows what those are, knows how to discover them in potential hires, and never veers from that path.

Taking hiring one step into the future, when a Great Workplace finds that after a short time, or even over the long term, a hire shows NOT to be The Right Person Doing the Right Things Right, they correct that mistake; quickly, and without hassle.

The number one reason The Right People leave an organization is *"bad management"* (not benefits or pay). An organization could have in place all the right methods of attracting The Right People (including benefits and pay), but has not developed those people internally who can affect retention. Those *"bad managers"* show the Right People being hired, that the organization does NOT have an integrated value system, or an ongoing intent to have The Right People Doing the Right Things, Right.

A brief example: The Great Workplace 2.0 was asked by a client of our search firm to come in and discuss why this third-generation manufacturing company was experiencing horrible retention of shop and engineering personnel and had developed a reputation in the candidate community as a *"place NOT to work."* After very basic probing, the owner admitted having two *"ogre-management-style"* shop managers who had been with the organization over 20 years, and simultaneously having an ineffective engineering staff (also high turnover). They also had less than engaging Human Resource people who treated potential hires like commodities. Their spoken intent was to change that, first by redefining their core values (they had none published except ISO quality adherence) and then by implementing a structured methodology of re-immersing current people to a *"new deal"*. We have not heard back from them on our proposal to facilitate and train on the evolution, and if anything, they are experiencing an even higher turnover rate in their shop. Sales are keeping them in business, but imagine the cost of the turnover and the mounting frustrations in productivity.

The next step to hiring and retaining The Right People doing The Right Things, Right is the Immersion process. Immersion is NOT a choice. It is a necessity for The Great Workplace. The TOP Great Workplaces build this into the recruiting process, not waiting for a person to actually begin work. The actual immersion process starts not after hire, but in the initial recruiting process, be that advertisements, internal referrals, direct recruiting, and especially with a third party search firm. Smart. Effective. And profitable. Immersion is so critical to creating The Great Workplace 2.0, we have given Immersion its own chapter. Immersion is where *"Connect, Engage, Collaborate"* begins.

Tools

Executive Summary:
- Tools conjure the vision of mechanical items, but it should not stop there. Tools encompasses not only mechanical or physical items needed to perform functions, but knowledge, development training, skills development and supportive non-tangible assets that allow the individual or Participant to become productive, as quickly as possible, and stay productive.
- In The Great Workplaces, Tools are planned; assets are accumulated and are available on a timely basis.
- To a Participant, the end result is Remarkable, and inspiring. An Inspired Participant achieves results.

Marshall McLuhan (twentieth-century author whose works advanced the concept of "Tools" as fundamental in the evolution of mankind (ex: The Gutenberg Galaxy). He wrote: "We shape our tools. And then our tools shape us." McLuhan was referring to the fact that our social practices co-evolve with our use of new tools and the refinements we make to existing tools (expansion from Wikipedia). Nothing could be more fitting for the Tools that Remarkable Organizations develop and implement as part of their entire strategy. We shape our Tools according to our purpose(s) knowing that these Tools leverage our own skills and knowledge. Tools help us achieve objectives, and those tools evolve as our uses for them evolve.

Let's assume that your business cards, internet access, training materials and company information all that one needs to start a new position is read and available for you day one. Even not-so-Great Workplaces get that.

Then the Tools are all the items and *"pools of Intelligence"* needed for a new person (or vendor/ board member/ contractor) to achieve defined performance objectives. On occasion, if these are not readily available or delivery has been delayed, there can be workarounds. But there is no good excuse for not having all the tools available that can be made available, PRIOR to commencement of the relationship. There are TOO many downsides for both parties in not being prepared.

The Great Workplaces assure the availability of Tools. It is a component of immersion, and immersion is the force behind alignment which quickly results in productivity.

"Pools of intelligence" is simply a fancy term used in this book to encompass all data-based works the new participant will need to get their hands on. Someone close to the Immersion process needs to know EXACTLY where those can be found, and access needs to be prearranged. Blue Prints? Available. Machine instructions? At the machine. Accounts Payable's recent run? Check the "In" box. Last quarter's financials? Locked up in THAT cabinet, I have the key...and so on.

Tools also mean that the Right People doing the immersion need to be planned, provided with their own tools and are in the right frame of mind to accomplish the objectives of Immersion. They will also need input from the hiring team as to how best approach the new Participant. How will this person best learn? What are they used to? Generation X? Vietnam-era generation? Although this is a component of the Immersion strategy itself, it needs to be discussed as a way to be a tool and to provide tools to the new participant. The Tool is Immersion, How we form and evolve that Tool determines success.

As a Recruiter, I visited a client who eventually became an interviewee for The Great Workplace 2.0. We first talked about the expected results for the person-to-be-hired to achieve. After about an hour of discussing the *"Why's"* we got into the *"How's."* That's when the discussion got Remarkable: The hiring authority proceeded to SHOW me EXACTLY what this person would do (in the short version of the long plan).

He took me through each defined duty, showed me the *"field manual"* for each, walked me through each function, showed me each department where interaction would take place, introduced me to each Manager, and took an example *"form"* that would be used in the job as it went through the process. It didn't stop there. He showed me *"Intelligence Pools"* (Reference materials) that were available, showed me training and development guides that would be taught by others, and the "Tour" went on for over an hour.

At each step, the organization had planned and made available not only written guidance, but online assets that were to be at the call of the new employee. There were a lot of *"If the person needs _____, here is where they need to look."*

Tools were completely available, development was planned, and the path to success was clearly laid out. At each juncture, we discussed the areas where improvements were expected and would be noticed. It may seem that this position was one of simple *"processes"* that any person of average intelligence could follow. The instructions though showed where *"judgment"* and individual creativity were needed and used.

But as Remarkable as the map was, it was eclipsed by the explanations of *"Why"* each function was critical, and *"Why"* improvements were critical to the entire organization. If I may talk out of school a tad: The hiring authority also pointed out the built-in areas of people and direction contentions (the hills to climb). No pre-judgment was involved, no drama put on the table. Just the hurdles to jump, and areas to be addressed.

This alone made the evaluation of potential successful candidates a ton easier, but not *"easy."* Candidate Values and Ideas had to be vetted. Character had to be discovered. The result was that I and my firm could focus on finding The Right Person, and explaining the tools available that would help in their success.

After about three weeks in his new assignment, the successful hire called me to tell me that the organization's roadmap (plan, tools, immersion) "Blew his mind." He had never worked for an organization as prepared to help achieve success as this organization. He was pumped, directed and ready to tackle the world.

Tools, and all that means, inspire and connect with The Right People so that they can Do The Right Things, Right.

Now, the opposite example: Again, a client hired our recruiting firm to look for a highly-skilled shop technical person. Someone who had 15-years of specific experience, and the client was willing to pay for it. We thoroughly understood the position, the results expected, and had a great tour of the facilities. We successfully found the "Right" person (of course!).

After three days the new hire called us, and wanted to know what kind of game was being played? The expected onboarding of products, technology, tools and culture never took place. The person designated for this was not available. After being hardly spoken to the first morning, even by the HR person, he was given a print and told to "make the process, make the part." Okay, he thought, maybe this was some of the training. On his own he found the programs, designed the process with a little help from a guy in the department. Being told to "make it" he went to the shop floor and asked around for direction. You guessed it: no idea where to start.

The outcome was not bad, however, even though the person was ready to call his old employer and beg to come back. With the president's help that next morning (we got him on his mobile at a soccer match that evening), direction was given, tools (literally) were explained, assets were identified and a path was agreed to. Other heads rolled and new Immersion and Asset awareness programs were implemented, but just for this one person. He is now in charge of other people like himself and is working on a true "time-to-productivity" plan, for the entire organization, working directly with the owner.

Communication Channels are tools.
Both internal and external. Channels for communication need to be two-way, open, easy to work with and responsive. The old *"Suggestion Box"* has new and more productive iterations.

Communication Channels as Tools:
Remarkable Organizations encourage open and immediate exchange of information, ideas and actions that can or will affect the ability of Participants to meet objectives and Purpose(s). Open communication channels can prevent knowledge *"siloing"* (knowledge or ideas or feedback secured in a privately controlled

container), which is very common in organizations without Shared Purpose or an open collaborative culture. Siloing typically happens when individual performance is regarded above the good of the whole, where there is a weak alignment of all participants to Purpose, and/or when Transparency is avoided. This stems from an us-versus-them mentality or from a *"Me"* mentality, which in most cases is fomented by the organization's (lack of?) structure or Leadership. In those cases fear, survival and selfish behaviors have become dominant forces. Remarkable Organizations reduce individual tendencies by having a firm Purpose to the organization, and purposeful tools at hand. Lest you get the wrong idea, this is not a rigid dictatorship ordering directives to automatons. Think of it as the garden hose that directs the water stream.

Most small- to medium-size organizations do not, by necessity, have a borderless workplace. Those that do have work-at-home participants, contractors, remote call centers, remote collaborative workplaces and field agents, and customers who need to be connected to the *"Mother Ship"* have designed unique systems (Tools) to Connect all of those wide-reaching assets so that it seems a close environment.

Real-time video, audio and messaging are just a few of the Communication Channels being used. Internet Whiteboarding, a Collaborative project management software system, is another tool commonly used, as are real-time applications that are resident on Smartphones and tablets. I will not go into the exact brands being used, but if you need to have efficient state-of-the-art communications with remotely based participants, the tools available will boggle your mind. Star Trek officers would be jealous.

Other useful and well-disseminated tools involve customer and supplier feedback channels. The Remarkable organization provides direct-line private feedback via phone, Internet sites and Linked order/supplier/provider software that can follow an order from inception to delivery, even allowing production or design updates in the process, through to quality feedback from the customer. When linked to Quality standards, feedback produces necessary or required actions on the part of suppliers and producers to find root causes for issues and produce solution feedback.

Those state-of-the-art, looped feedback systems should NOT stop at physical productivity. Remarkable Organizations practice open communications in much the same manner.

Collaborative Alignment begins with every Participant understanding their roles in delivering on the Purpose of the organization, which starts with the Immersion process, and never stops. Each participant also understands the roles of others in the organization and teams or departments and understands the roles of other teams and departments and how to support or positively influence those efforts. Each will understand the importance in Collaborative efforts for the ultimate goals of the organization.

By aligning roles, accountabilities, Collaborative and teamwork expectations with the Integrated Operating Plan and Values, the path to Purpose becomes clear and the natural tendencies toward silos is dramatically reduced. The effect is Transparency; everyone knows the same expectations and which path to follow.

Opening all communications creates a focus on the Customer, and therefore a less encumbered path to the organization's Purpose.

Remarkable Organizations reward Collaborative Efforts publically. Teams get recognition. Collaborations (groups) are heralded. Recognition is supported by the organization's Leadership, and team leaders.

Newsletters, on paper and online, use current events, Team accomplishments and Collaborations to support the organization's Valuing Open Communication as a Tool for achieving Purpose. Departmental and inter-departmental meetings not only discuss needed projects and results, but the value of open communications in achieving goals.

Leaders, having the image of walking "Tools" of open communication, typically update units and departments on current happenings and use THE most powerful question to facilitate open and meaningful communications:

"What do YOU think?"

The power in that question comes from proving that what a single person or subordinate leader has to offer, is of great importance to the entire organization. Of course, the thoughts of others cannot be casually dismissed, and great Leaders ask more questions to the original answer so that they fully understand. Great Leaders know that their response to the answers either encourage continuing open communications or stop it dead in the tracks by dismissing the answer, therefore the person.

Open communication channels Inspire Participants to do more and achieve. There is no single, proper path to Open, Collaborative and Transparent communications for any organization. Achieving it as a Tool does however require that the Values of the organization, the Operating Plan and the guidance given to Participants Align with the Purpose of the organization and that *"Lip Service"* is not a part of perception from Participants. Keep it real. Keep it open. Keep it valued. Development of Participant skills is a powerful Tool.

ALL owners, managers and Human Resource Professionals want their participants to grow in their capabilities. That means that the organization can grow and Endure. In the rush of everyday business operations this desire gets side-tracked more often than not.

Remarkable Organizations KNOW that when a Participant is given personal or institutional development opportunities that person feels Valued, is more likely to be Productive and feel a direct "Connection" to the organization. Skill development Engages participants beyond identification with the organization itself; it opens participants' eyes to the organization's and their own future. Just ask any job candidate what they want for their future and most will respond: *"I want to grow, learn new things and advance with the company."* Beyond the fact that many job candidates use that phrasing as a required litany during an interview, for The Right People, it is very true. The challenge is to find people who see Growing is an Opportunity, not simply an expectation to be given and measured by some supervisory person, and therefore having reduced value. Refer to our chapter in this book: *"The Right People Doing the Right Things, Right®."*

The typical organization today wants to hire an individual who can *"hit the ground running"* and attempts to match a job description with a candidate's skill set. Once the person is hired and pointed in the right direction, then it is often 'hands-off' as the person is left to achieve expected results. Later, following that model, an organization is surprised and feels discontented that the person is doing the same things, the same way many months after they started. They expected the individual to figure the rest (growth) out on their own. It rarely happens that way.

The Remarkable organization plans an extended Immersion from *"Start to Retirement"* for each *"job"* function within the organization. This may sound tiresome and difficult to predict. It really is not. Remarkable Organizations have astute managers analyze the growth and productivity curves for functions reporting to them for common ceilings and plateaus, and plan Development (Improvement) initiatives to correlate with those benchmarks. These initiatives include re-training sessions, sideways promotions, outside schooling, interim assignments for the individual to train or develop others (a great way to refresh skills and motivation is to have an individual prepare to teach their knowledge, skills and abilities to others), interim projects to re-challenge people, and counseling sessions with higher-level executives and professional HR practitioners.

The results of *"Cradle To Grave"* development planning is Remarkable; turnover becomes more predictable due to closer monitoring of performance progress and attitude *"checks."* Participants' desires to contribute in different ways are discovered and encouraged, ambitions can be sparked, objective contributions can be more closely directed and skill training needs can be uncovered and administered.

In other words; the proper Tools can be formed, evolved and applied to all human and intangible assets within the organization when they are needed. Remarkable Organizations take even better care of Human Assets than they do physical ones. Machines rarely walk out the front door, people do.

Immersion (Onboarding)

Executive Summary:

- Quite simply, The Great Workplace 2.0 does a better (Remarkable) job of Engaging new talent AND Participants to the organization and reaps larger paybacks than those organizations who that do not Onboard or those that use the legacy style of *"Orientation."*

- Immersion shortens the new Participant's time to productivity. It Engages a participant more deeply into the performance expectations of the organization, and it Aligns the entire horsepower of the organization's engine directly to its Purpose, Missions and goals. If you are not doing this, your 8-cylinder engine is functioning on 4.

- The Immersion process creates a common future for all participants by aligning the organization's performance expectations, Values, Purpose and Missions to the participant's talents and aspirations. It is done in a strategically planned and executed fashion to shorten a new hire's time to productivity.

- Immersion is a two-way collaborative learning process to be delivered by a select group of practical visionaries within your organization, not the most convenient.
- Design the process to be a Remarkable Experience and it will achieve Remarkable Results.

The Great Workplace 2.0 invokes an *"Immersion"* process that exceeds the traditional Onboarding scheme. In the past, organizations did *"Orientation."* Many still do. Organizations that just do Orientation are not considered The Great Workplace 2.0.

We define *"Orientation"* as the quick process designed to show a participant what they are expected to do and with whom. This is typically assigned to a first-line supervisor or when that supervisor is busy, it is administered by a senior employee in or near the department in which the new employee will working. In some cases it is accomplished by a Human Resource representative. Many of us will remember, *"Here's the lunchroom, here's the payroll office, here are some videos to watch, here's your desk"* speech. Not Thrilling.

Orientation accomplishes the **least** an organization can afford to accomplish. It literally *"introduces"* the individual to the organization and then relies upon a natural process of socialization (leave it to chance) to take over from there. A problem with minimal socialization is the lack of trust that an existing employee has with a new employee (*"Is he here to take my job?"*) and *"what's the new guy going to do?"* There is no alignment with the existing community of participants, and certainly not with the organization's Purpose. In most cases orientation is simply a way of letting the new participant get a *"feel"* for the environment, while supervisors do their jobs.

Immersion is "Creating A Common Future."

The goal of immersing a new participant is to set the foundation for a successful relationship by creating a Common Future. Thorough Immersion builds Connection, Engagement and Collaboration. It builds a Shared Trust and a Shared Community through exposure, pollination, awareness and education.

It can build nothing short of a contemporary, collaborative *"Tribal"* organization. At its center is a social and ideological foundation for solidarity. And yet, each time a *"Participant"* is added to the organization, the makeup or strength of the future is slightly modified. It flows. It gains strength.

Done well, onboarding builds upon the strengths of the entire organization through individuals and through Community. Attempted poorly or not at all, it assures that the individual and the organization have begun their association at arm's length. Visualize two Heisman trophies facing each other. (Note for non-footballers: the Heisman Trophy depicts a football runner sticking his arm out to ward off tacklers, straight-arm style. As if to say, "Go Away! You're not going to touch me.

Onboarding is a STRATEGIC PROCESS designed to attract, engage and acclimate new Talent to an organization quickly. It is meant to reaffirm their decision to join the organization (eliminate buyer's remorse), Connect and Engage individuals into the organization's culture (values in action) and point each individual in the direction of career, and therefore, organization success (performance expectations).

It is a retention tool. It is also a tool that can identify miss-hires quickly or redirect skills to needed areas (there are NO perfect hiring selection methods).

It is discovery, for both the organization and individual. In the immersion process just as much is learned about the individual or external participant (Vendors, board, community) as is learned about the organization itself.

It is an all-hands-oriented Integration system and an extension of an externally oriented Selection system.

Onboarding at The Great Workplace 2.0 level is the beginning of Innovation and Collaboration.

An Onboarding system also contains the ability for the organization to use a central point to distribute and collect employment-related forms, tasks, insurance claims, corporate information and much more. That is the *"Administrative"* purpose of Onboarding. The payoff is when this process is strategic.

To a legacy organization (old ideas, old styles), Onboarding is a chore focused on new hires—although smart organizations go as far as Onboarding people who are promoted within the organization or who change responsibilities. It is a chore due in many ways to payback being seen as ONLY a future event, not as a flowing foundation process.

Great consulting organizations like Taleo, Towers, and McKinsey stress mechanization of the Onboarding process to facilitate the social fabric necessary to make onboarding a thorough process of connection. Forms and benefits and stories are combined with mechanized hand-holding of a new member so that existing members do not have to spend an inordinate amount of their valuable time explaining and re-explaining the organization to new members, nor are there gaps in or inaccuracies in the messages given that could lead to confusion or litigation. New members have the maximum time to get the lay of the land, to ask questions in a neutral non-pressurized atmosphere with an experienced employee dedicated to the purpose.

But organizations that do not have the cash to achieve mechanization can actually out-do the big guys. After all, *"It's not how big you are, but how Remarkable."* They can apply a *"high-touch"* twist to even the mundane.

In today's world of fringe participants and dichotomous messages, Great Workplaces use Immersion as a necessary tool in protecting itself from corporate terrorists, i.e., extremists out to get **for themselves** through workers' compensation, litigation or infiltration.

The Great Workplaces of today and tomorrow realize that ANY Participant can affect the success of their organization and endeavor to thoroughly indoctrinate and connect with them at a level beyond: *"Here's what we do, here's what you do."* Immersion is also being extended to Full Participant Lifecycle: a process that leads the participant throughout and beyond their connection to the organization itself.

Immersion accelerates payback:
The Great Workplaces have transformed Onboarding into Immersion. It forces the deep dive quickly, through as many channels as possible. It provides as much philosophy and purpose as it does mechanization. It connects people who otherwise would not be connected.

It builds Shared Culture through defined values and performance expectations (Culture is *"Values in Action"*). It builds the platform for Innovation. It builds the ability of any participant for engagement with the Customer's satisfaction. It pollinates the diversity of ideas and points of view necessary to take a divergent group of participants and gives them a *"meeting place"* in their minds (Purpose).

It quite simply reduces the time for a new Participant to payback the investment the organization has made. Remarkable Immersion processes focus on the knowledge, comfort level and targeted results needed in a fashion that allows little *"filler"* time.

What Are The Best Organizations Stressing In Immersion?

Even before a new participant is hired, the best organizations set the framework for immersion. It begins with Career Advertising, website information, immersion of third-party recruiters and with internal sources of employee referral.

Website information: this is a much-missed opportunity to educate career-seeking individuals about the organization, and if that is missing, the *"passive"* job seeker looking for reasons to pursue a "better opportunity" is given no reason to even make an inquiry, much less an application for employment.

Proper and attractive website information regarding why people want to work, stay and thrive there is critical to attracting talent. This is THE opportunity to provide marketing-style information on Values, Purpose, Culture and Expectations. Most companies still consider a website as the place for product information and a brief *"About Us"* column that states things like date founded, markets served, products made (the what and the how) and some brief statements about *"customer service is essential"* or future intentions (Missions). This is your first opportunity to align your entire organization's expectations and rewards with future participant's aspirations and values. Immersion is all about alignment, and it does not start on the first day of employment or first exercise of job functions. If you don't think potential customers will read your website to discover who you are, you are fooling yourself. They want to know not only the What and How, but the Why. Why is not only answered directly in their questions to you, but in how you present yourself to the public.

One of our TOP Great Workplaces has a mediocre-looking website, until one gets into the guts of it. It extols their values, culture, history and future. It has videos on their unique technology AND it has a video of the founder/ CEO talking about the company, employee expectations, culture and future. Amazingly, it is not scripted, just from the heart. It sells.

Another TOP Great Workplace CEO came into our studio to record a video directed at potential and current employees regarding expectations, new service introductions and his ideas for the success of the organization. With no notes, and little preparation, he stepped onto the stage and gave a mesmerizing 5-minute, animated "WHY for the customer and employee" chat. Our studio personnel applauded his message and delivery. As you might expect, this organization is a perennial Weatherhead 100, Fast Growth Company award-winner, among numerous other individual and industry awards they and their founder have achieved. They are able to attract top talent and retain them.

The organization's story. Every organization has one. It is the legacy, but it is still growing. It is the Who, What, How and Why that brought the organization to today. It is the hard work that has been done. It is the people who have done it. It is the foundation of the future, even if the story is only three months old. It is an inspiration for today and beyond, even if there are issues. Open the closet, but also show how and why things have changed or are changing. Honesty is key. Excuses are not. If you don't have a story to tell, then you don't have an operating plan, and you have no true values, or you have little integrity (no real Purpose). Either correct that or fold up shop. You have, at best, a rotten job that you should probably leave (as the owner) right after lunch.

An example story; I include this example here because Membership in an organization is very much a Concept based upon the Story of the organization's past and future. Although there are tangible benefits members will receive, there is no physical or touchable product like in a manufacturing organization.

One of the TOP Entrepreneurs Associations in the United States, John Carroll University's Entrepreneurs Association (250 Members, minimum requirements are: 5 years in business, $1 million in annual sales, member must be a principal owner) invoked a thorough Immersion Process for all new members, while encouraging existing members to attend the process.

This 3+ hour intense immersion explains each area of the organization (presented by each board committee chair), what that unit does, with whom, why and their results. It delves deeply into the history of the organization, the progress made FOR MEMBERS, and for the organization. It lays out the future. It explains what the member can expect by being involved in any of the units, what benefits members will receive from learning events, and what is expected of each involved member. The Immersion process is founded upon the organization's Purpose (and Missions) and it stresses the common and shared future.

This organization is not one for a casual entrepreneur. The average member organization does about $13 million in annual sales. Gray hair is as common as not, and women make up a growing percentage of the membership. The JCUEA connects directly with students at John Carroll and members give freely and formally of their experience and wisdom. In its first year, the Immersion process at JCUEA has made a remarkable and tangible difference in the engagement of this experienced and somewhat Prove it to me-oriented group of achievers. If you think an immersion process may be difficult for new employees, think about herding a large group of cats (i.e., experienced and successful Owners). That is what the JCUEA has achieved under the leadership of the uniquely experienced Mark Hauserman, Director: a Common Future (www.jcuea.org).

Integrated Operating Plan, including an organizational chart. What a unit, person, group or vendor organization does what, how and why. How do units, people and the outside world Integrate and Collaborate for the organization's Purpose and Missions. What are the *"connectors"* (the top of the Tipi) that make everything work? What will this new person or organization have to do to achieve Performance Expectations? Define the role. Define what success looks like, the positive affects success has on the whole. Define how failure affects each connection and the whole. Define good, great, remarkable. To be brutally honest, without this deep dive for a new employee or vendor, they are lost and feel insignificant. And if that is how you want them to feel, that is how they will perform.

The performance results expectations that have been introduced throughout the hiring process are now taken down to a functional level. These expectations are laid out in a collaborative way in terms of goals, duties, measurable performance results and time frames. They are tied to review benchmarks, timelines and quality-oriented guidelines. There should be no questions about expectations moving forward. This needs to be handled by direct supervisors and unit Managers.

Tools for success are introduced. ANY asset that will be used by the Participant is introduced in the Immersion process. This however does not mean that future training on that asset's actual use must be done in the first week, unless it will be used immediately. Immersion, strategically planned, may take up to six months to complete. But the introduction of tools to be used is done as needed. Knowing what tools will be available and when, will ease a Participant's concern about *"How am I going to get these things done?"*

Vendors and outside Collaborators get Immersion: The Great Workplaces can and will steal your best vendors. You will demand of all outside participants their absolute best, including but not limited to price. But there is a significant and remarkable difference between The Great Workplaces and the *"almost great"*: The Great Workplaces intuitively and by design KNOW that a vendor can either make or break some missions and assist in reaching goals. So, what they do is Immerse potential vendors as they would an employee, as part of their vetting process. They encourage the vendor to give advice, not just product, and they encourage the vendor to become engaged in the success of the partnership.

Typical buyers in non-remarkable workplaces give little, demand price reductions and do not encourage collaborations. They put vendors at arm's length, treating them as kids at Thanksgiving Dinner: they send them over to the kid's table, away from the deserving adults and are told to *"Behave!"* Great Workplaces realize that if you want someone's best (with a vendor, it almost always comes down to a "someone") you treat them that way. They ask questions relative to capabilities, knowledge of product innovations in the marketplace and when what is being purchased is a *"How-To"* they probe deeply and drink heavily of the knowledge the vendor can share. In essence they ask the most critical question not-so-great workplace people don't ask: *"What do YOU think?"*

Provide a senior executive meet-up. Really smart Great Workplaces provide an audience with at least one Decision Maker. It does not have to be a half day affair. But the dialogue must be meaningful and purposeful. There is no excuse for NOT doing this is a smaller organization, regardless of the level of position. What this shows is Visible, Tangible Leadership. It is like meeting Coach K at the Olympics. *"This man cared enough about ME, to take the time to talk."* It shows the organization is serious about their commitment to Participants. The best meeting happens when the Executive is prepared by knowing WHO the individual or the group of new people is, by name and background. The executive is prepared to ask questions: *"Why are you joining us?" "What can we expect of you?" "What do you expect of us?" "What questions can I answer?"* And that executive needs to be prepared to chat about the organization, its purpose, missions, culture and values. In that way, the new participant sees and hears the connection of the *"sold"* characteristics of the organization, to the reality. It is Connect, Engage and Collaborate at the foundation.

A side story: I was a new hire at Capital American Insurance Group in the 1980s. At that time it was a high-intensity, high-growth organization, full of amazing talent. On my second day at *"The Cap"*, I was moved into a closet-sized office (no other was available due to physical expansion) with a desk that barely fit and a single chair in front of it sort of hanging out the door due lack of space. I was studying product literature in preparation for a meeting with the VP of Underwriting. A small, professorial man appeared in this small doorway and asked if he could spend a few minutes with me. Only after a few minutes did he introduce himself as Barry Hershey, with no title and no pomp. He was the owner/ chairman and genius behind the success of The Cap, then a professor at Harvard. He had grown the company from an agency to an underwriter of specialty insurance products about to fly past $300 million in annual sales and a worth of about the same. Barry later sold the company to Canseco for about $500 million.

Needless to say I gulped. My opportunity to make a first impression, I hoped I wasn't about to blow it. To my surprise Barry wanted to ask my opinion about the little I knew about Capital American. We spent the next two hours talking about the company history, Barry and myself as individuals, my opinions on what the company could do in the future. I was ENGAGED and committed. When Barry left, the next apparition in my miniscule office was David Lazar, company president. At the end of the day I not only needed a nap, but a shower. I was committed.

The truth. If you don't bring the good, the bad and the Remarkable to the table, in the right perspective, don't think that it won't be found out quickly. And you won't be there to correct any negative reaction to it. Try as we might in The Great Workplace, there will always be one person who will in fact find the newbie and fill that person with their own personalized version of whining. Most right people will ignore the bad apple, but the damage will have been done, and questions will linger. This is especially true if Immersion is done by someone just going through the motions (you wouldn't do that, would you?). Every organization has challenges. That is also why you have an Integrated Business Plan that addresses those challenges in the right perspectives. That is a great reason to share that plan.

The Great Workplaces choose the Right People to do the connecting.

Immersion is not the *"property"* of Human Resources, if HR is purely involved in compliance activities. Compliance is rules and regulations. Immersion is engaging. But if HR is up for the challenge, I say go for it. Regardless of the depth and breadth of your Immersion process, you will need to choose a team of individuals who are more than visionary and are completely capable of Connecting, Engaging and Collaborating on all levels, not simply reading from prepared text. Allow those people the time, uninterrupted, to achieve the Purpose of your immersion process. It can be exhausting, and due to the focus, it can be a process of discovery. You will discover a wealth of information about the person or organization being immersed. The people involved need to be astute enough to recognize potential issues with the target, not just do the process. It should be a TEAM of people, right down to the direct supervisor. And it will take time. Immersion is not a one-day activity. It might take weeks or months. And it is worth it.

Assign a mentor. Mentors are carefully chosen in The Great Workplaces as the Guiding Lights for new participants. These Right People are chosen for their own immersion into the inner workings of the organization, the Values, Purposes, Missions and knowledge of reality. The Mentor does NOT HAVE TO BE in the new person's direct area, but should be knowledgeable of all facets of the organization, including personalities, red tape, illusions to be made into reality and a reiteration of the *"Game Plan"* for the organization. The Mentor is assigned to be a confidant or mirror for the person and organization. They can answer questions that many new participants won't be comfortable asking of their direct supervisor or team in immersion. Those questions may even be based in confusion of material covered or something that simply was not grasped. Choose the Mentor carefully and Immerse that person in expectations. Mentorship needs to know the difference between acceptable confidentiality and practical cautions.

Successful Immersion takes a plan. *"Orientation"* does not. Orientation can be done in an hour. The lunch room doesn't move very often. That is one reason why it doesn't work. Immersion should be strategic, with assignments for the immersion process and job duties in place. It needs to be orderly. One facet leads to the next and there is logic to it. It cannot be accomplished by itself. Productive Onboarding of an employee needs time for that person to digest the importance and content. And it needs to start before the actual hire, so that it is a flowing sequence of intelligence.

Immersion requires feedback. Is the material being understood and consumed? What opinions does this person have now? How can the concepts be applied? What is expected of this person? How can you improve the process? Does the person truly agree with the content and the concepts? Do they see how the material relates to their position/role?

What has been left out? Certainly targeted job function training (we assume this will get done), the *"rules"* of being an employee, parking spaces, expense reimbursements, benefits, workers' compensation, safety training, intellectual property, contracts and human behaviors, and the like. Some of this belongs under *"Administration."* The Great Workplace 2.0 covers all of those with aplomb.

Why Some Organizations Hesitate About True Immersion.
The most common responses to this are predictable: Small staff with little time to spend on immediately non-productive activities. Everyone is swamped. We'll fill in organizational stories and values as the person gets trained to do the job. If we spend all that time in Onboarding, and the person does not work out, it will be time totally wasted. The new person will find out all the ancillary things about the organization as they go.

The facts are that **Fear** and a focus on today's activities drive many good organizations away from total Immersion processes. The Fear is about many things: We don't have a completely solid organization, yet. We are working on things. If we expose that to new people or Vendors, they will lack confidence in us. I'm not sure I have people in place who can accomplish the process with expertise.

Solution: You have to start somewhere. Design the process around the best of what you have, and know that not only will the process get better, but so will the organization. Trust your best people. Immerse them first. Ask for a collaborative solution, and oversee the first several immersions so you are certain they *"get it."*

Here is the real fear: We can't do this because we have no written or agreed upon Values, Purpose, identifiable Culture or Integrated Operating Plan. We have existed without those or we are new.

Solution: Start with the 13 Characteristics of The Great Workplace 2.0. Take the time to build your Tipi. Build your Purpose, Values and Operating Plan. Make these things real. While you are doing this, by yourself if need be, or in a collaborative effort with your most trusted team members, Immerse existing participants as fully as possible, and roll out an Immersion Strategy. Eventually your Immersion plan will take on a life of its own and will reflect your foundation, and you will be on your way to becoming Remarkable!

Remember: Create a common future for all participants by aligning your performance expectations with corporate Values, Purpose and Missions to the participant's talents and aspirations. Do so in a strategically planned and executed fashion to shorten the time to productivity. Immersion is a two-way collaborative learning process to be delivered by a select group of practical visionaries within your organization, not the most convenient. Design the process to be a Remarkable Experience and it will achieve Remarkable results

Collaboration: The Great Workplace 2.0 Flourishes on a Collaborative Culture

Executive Summary:

- None of us as business owners or executives have all the solutions to issues, nor all the Innovations needed to compete in today's global economy, even if we operate a local-only business. We need a group of ideas, not the same ideas, to move us forward.
- Teamwork will get us part of the way, but we are then only as good as our team, and only as creative as the lowest-to-medium common denominator of that team.
- Collaboration breeds the ideas and innovations that we need, and the results can be *Remarkable*.

By definition, The Great Workplace is committed to fostering a collaborative, productive, engaging and rewarding culture that encompasses customers, prospective employees, employees, vendors, Participants (Stake/ Shareholders) and the community. The organization practices collaboration to the extent that Internal and external no longer have a distinction, and it recognizes that Community has no true boundaries.

Here are two facts about Collaboration as a strategic business tool that may keep you reading, especially if you are of the legacy mentality (*"Prove to me this new fangled stuff works!"*):

1) The #1 consumer products company in the USA has seen products that were developed by EXTERNAL collaborations grow from 15 percent of sales to 35 percent of sales. And 45 percent of new products have elements in their development due to EXTERNAL collaborations. That equates to Tens of BILLIONS of dollars of sales and BILLIONS of dollars of profit. These new products were NOT bought or acquired; they were developed from a strategic collaborative process.

2) The # 1 Healthcare hardware organization in The USA FELL to a level of 55 percent fulfillment rate of their orders because they LOST the majority of their vendors to the recession and their own lack of "touch" (Collaboration) with those vendors. When their fulfillment rate fell to a critical level, the company was NOT AWARE of the percentage of vendor die-offs. They did not have Collaboration as part of their culture. Their vendors were handled at arm's length. The organization knew everything and could do anything, including treat their vendors like step-children. Even those vendors that survived the recession are re-thinking IF they want to do business with this company again. Losing a vendor is NOT very different than losing a knowledge base.

"Collaboration" is defined here, for our purposes, as: *Uniting disparate entities or assets that may have different individual purposes (or goals) and aligning them for a single purpose or goal that may NOT be their first defined responsibility or accountability.*

Collaboration is NOT teamwork, although it may feel that way. Collaboration is NOT simply getting a bunch of people together in a room and asking their opinion, as legacy organizations seem to do.

Collaboration is the view that the enterprise has an extended base of knowledge and expertise and this extended base SHOULD be used for solutions, direction and innovations. Collaboration is by nature OPEN and at the same time integrated. It is an evolution of thought that is put into play, even though in our *"Command and Control"* world, the very nature of collaboration will seem counter-intuitive.

Collaboration is a strategic tool that demands the enterprise make visible the assets of the enterprise.

Collaboration dictates that the Marlboro Man (the image of the Lone Ranger, so to speak) must be retired, and the new hero is an ever-changing group of talent. Top Talent or in the terms of Characteristics of The Great Workplace 2.0 is The Right People Doing the Right Things, Right. These *"Right People"* are or should be collaborative by nature, they seek to understand, not first to be understood (Jim Collins). Collaborative people know that they do not know everything, and are constantly seeking great ideas, innovative thoughts and dreams generated by anyone and everyone, and can filter those ideas and innovations according to Purpose.

Collaboration IS or can be structured, strategic, planned and at the same time…chaotic (Collaboration is in fact to many people a true dichotomy of concepts). The chaos is defined by having non-linear thinking CONVERGING into the creative process. Lack of chaos almost always points to a lack of divergent thinking, therefore a more predictable and manageable outcome (legacy). Collaboration understands that IF the organization KNEW the outcome before the process was initiated, then the process itself is flawed, and the collaboration was simply a false attempt.

You own a car. A nice one at that. You spent much time nursing your Credit Score, saving money and budgeting your cash flow so that you could buy that new ride. You brought it home and admired it. The neighbors admired it, and so did your kids.

Now, go into the garage, pop the hood and disconnect three of the six or eight sparkplug leads so that your car uses only three of the six or eight cylinders it came with. It now spurts and pops and chugs. It can be driven, just not as well as it could or should. In some cases, it won't go at all. But hell, it uses less gas, and the ability of the vehicle to function is under your direct control.

Even though you know what you just did to your car, you may be doing the same thing to your own organization without knowing the direct cause and effect.

Cutting off customers, vendors, outside experts, your own employees, Board members, friends and acquaintances, let alone the wealth of the Internet may be identical to shutting down spark plugs in your car.

Legacy workplaces regularly cut off their ability to fully utilize all their competitive assets, just like in the example of your car. They do what is called *"SILO-ing"* their assets (putting them in a closed system). Especially the ones regularly at their door: their employees, vendors, advisors and community. These assets may seem less controllable or less linear in their orientation toward the ultimate success of the organization or the innovation of products and services. And, *"what do they know anyhow!"*

Collaboration finds its most friendly nests in organizations that need to be highly competitive, highly innovative and highly fluid to survive or thrive in their fields. And it seems that the more of a need to be innovative, the easier it is to convince management of a need for Collaborative culture.

In a collaborative environment, disparate (or *"cross functional"*) entities, with their own purposes are brought together to focus creative energies on a single activity that has its own Purpose or goal. The disparate entities align their own Purpose(s) for the stated Purpose (goal) of the collaborative assembly, and by achieving that Purpose or goal, allow their own *"Purpose"* to expand.

Collaboration extends Connectivity and Engagement to all *"Participants"* and in that way extends the reach of the enterprise beyond a single *"center"* for solutions. Remember that *"Participants"* includes insiders and outsiders who have a connection to and interest in the success of the organization.

In collaborative environments a unique, but highly productive non-activity happens: Through *Serendipity*, new opportunities, solutions and assets are found that were not seen before. Somewhat like searching behind the couch cushions for your car keys and finding a $5 bill. Serendipity is a propensity for making fortuitous discoveries while looking for something unrelated.

It is through the leveraging of this EXTENDED enterprise (Collaboratively bringing disparate entities together) that an organization can leverage tremendous assets it typically would ignore.

How does or can this work? Here is a real-life example: An organization that has about 120 employees in Northeast Ohio and does custom *"Identification"* solutions for companies (Product tags, printing, ID tags, etc) has setup up a room specifically for working WITH customers on new products or designing solutions for customer product issues. This room is chock full of previous examples of winning solutions for other customers, including POP displays. The meeting *"Tables"* are not round, nor square, but unique in shape. The room has been designed (high ceilings, glass, warm colors, open) to encourage creativity, but also crisp organization.

Brought into the meeting are:
- Customer Representatives
- 2 Company Designers
- 1 Person from Shipping
- 1 Person from Customer Service
- 1 Person from Accounting
- 1 person from a Main Material supplier
- Me (an outside vendor who has nothing to do with the product)
- The Receptionist

Everyone is given an explanation of what goal (or Purpose) the company's product has. Drawings are circulated, discussed, questions are asked. The designers have a format to follow that is one of *"discovery"* about the customer's customer.

What the customer wants this organization to design (achieve) is discussed and lots of fun ideas hit the table.

You know where this is going: Each individual at the table has a creative idea from THEIR POINT OF VIEW (Including me). The shipping guy talks about changing the design size to save money (serendipity). The materials vendor talks about new materials and manufacturing methods that could be used. He introduces a totally NEW material he would like to experiment with, just for this product.

Result: That day, the design and direction is highly creative, practical, and workable. The customer is ecstatic. The next meeting will be about a prototype, costs, etc.

Note: Ecstatic customer. VERY happy employees. VERY, VERY happy vendors.

2nd note: There were NO "managers" present. None. All people were staff level. The facilitator (The Receptionist) had a brief outline and 1 hour training on collaboration facilitation. She was thrilled.

Guess what the receptionist will tell customers who call in and want to chat?

Here is the lesson: In legacy companies, this meeting would never have happened. Only designers would be present, and the meeting would be *"conducted"* (See our chapter on *"Blues Jam"*) by a manager. Everything would have been controlled. There may have been a solid outcome, but in Collaboration, many more people would take Ownership of the outcome for the customer, including me. * It should be noted that I was NOT invited to the organization for this meeting. I happened to be visiting the president for a totally different purpose.

There are countless books on Collaboration, and more academic articles than needed to fill Lake Erie, so I won't bore you with more theory here.

Collaboration will not work as a daily methodology to run an organization. There still has to be one bus driver, and a crew of mechanics to keep it running. In fact, **Collaboration as an event** is unusual, and MUST be set up properly:

1) The participants to a collaborative event need to be chosen NOT for a Team effort, but for their unique or differing points of view.

2) The participants need to feel fully free to be creative, without recourse for unique or 'whacky' input.

3) The participants need to be fully educated on ultimate Purpose(s) for the collaboration, not on the expected or precise outcome. Their input should be directed toward innovation and creativity, not restating the obvious. Thinking *"out of the box"* is nurtured by *"getting rid of the box"*.

4) Participants need to focus on "giving everyone their due", and not getting their pleasures from judging other's ideas. This is True Tribal and comes from the Six Nations' (Ex: Iroquois) council meeting where everyone gets a voice and no one is permitted to criticize another. Interestingly, the methodology of the Council meeting is what our Congress was built from. The modern version of a council meeting entails the speaker holding the *"talking stick"* (too new age for business) where in the old days it was (and still is) an Eagle Feather. Don't try that. It is a $150,000 fine for those not permitted to have one.

5) The facilitator must be chosen with care as the skills necessary are not the same as Team Meetings or Ad-hoc *"what do you think"* sessions. The facilitator needs to be one who can keep and encourage the flow of ideas, and how one idea works off another. That person needs also to be able to let chaos flow and make sense of the diversions.

6) When a meeting comes to an end, the cumulative results and ideas need to be written and available to participants, for clarification and new thoughts. In this way, conclusions are less important than progress or new directions.

Continual Collaborations are of extreme value within The Great Workplace:

The Great Workplace uses a planned methodology of continual or continuous *"what do you think?"* type meet-ups with

ALL participants that are either continuous (ongoing but when necessary or advised) or continual (ongoing with no gaps, like ISO or Six Sigma methodology).

These take place as a matter of course within Remarkable Organizations and become part of the daily plan. It can be so prevalent that it is or can become its own Value for the organization: Innovation and Improvement, not only for the product or the service, but for the characteristics of that organization. It is in large part how The Great Workplaces Evolve, and in so doing, become Remarkable.

It also attracts the Right People. They want a hand in the Innovations for the future. It is both *"Potential"* and *"Realization"* to them. The challenges of the future, today. The Right People see Collaboration as a tool, and available supported tools mean career development. It means the ability to make a difference.

But this component of Collaboration needs to become part of the Culture of the organization, and in so doing proves its own Value or a component of a Value. It cannot be an afterthought or a timed project (Mission).

Continual Collaboration in The Great Workplace has these characteristics:

1) It has or is in process of becoming part of the Culture. *"What do you think?"* is not only sincere, but is acknowledged and expected.
2) When job duties and performance expectations are set, Continual Collaboration becomes a ritual. It is trained and developed. This exceeds the expected Teamwork protocol and becomes a core of Teamwork.
3) Continual Collaboration is built into the Operating Plan as all unit operating plans, to succeed, will necessitate

understanding how the Ultimate Purpose being achieved requires the flow of Collaborative thinking between disparate groups and missions.

4) Collaboration (continual or event) has the true backing of Visible, Tangible Leadership. The Leader doesn't just talk about it, but sanctions and supports it in his/her own activities.

Collaboration recognizes that answers, solutions and Innovations require open conversations with all Participants to the success of an organization. Collaborative environments SEEK the future today by utilizing every asset at their disposal, and creating new assets to continue improvements toward that future.

The organization that seeks and uses Collaboration as a component of their Culture is **Remarkable**. The alternative is simple: *"Crisis Management"* and continual fire-fighting are the Culture.

Collaboration is a Blues Jam

"Collaboration" is a characteristic of The Great Workplace of today and the future, and will be explained in business-detail in another excerpt. This chapter takes a lighter, but more pointed allegorical view of *"Collaboration"*:

> *"I got 29 ways to get in my baby's door. And if I need 'em, I can come up with two o' three more."*
>
> *(from a blues song by Tab Benoit)*

Have you ever been in a blues club when the owner called *"Open Stage/ Open Mic"* night? It is packed. Wall-to-wall audience. Wall-to-wall musicians waiting a turn. The hallways are packed. Every nook and cranny seems to have expanded to accommodate another body. Waitresses laugh, patrons laugh. Everybody seems to get into the act, to get into groove of the entire scene. Something good is happening here.

In the old days the smoke was so thick it redefined *"Second Hand."* Sometimes you wore your drink or the ice melted so fast, you just went along with the idea of sipping. The smells, oh, the smells! Only a few people got hammered. Takes too long to get a drink from the bar, even 20-feet away.

But the mood is always anticipation. Something new is going to happen. Maybe. Something innovative. Something no single group could ever devise on their own. Everyone is waiting for a *"Magic moment"* when the music is so good, you can feel it in your toes and bones. The players are in rapt anticipation of *"making new music"* that will flow from the talent and ideas of the moment, those they cannot experience playing only with their band.

People in the audience are there with their cases waiting for an opportunity to jam with people they just met. Some people have only a mouth harp in their pocket. Some just have a couple sticks. Others; just some ideas, a vocal riff and a few words to share.

Names are exchanged so quickly they are forgotten before the last vowel fades away into the noise from the juke. Singers stand staring into space rehearsing new verses to an old melody. The non-playing audience is frenetic, waiting to hear who is on, and who isn't. Waiting for that ultra special mixing bowl of talent to produce a one-of-a-kind, 5-minutes of music (during an all-night to early-morning session) that no one else, anywhere, at any time could reproduce. That 5 minutes of *"everything coming together"* leads into new songs, new combinations of talent(s), new groups, new music. New heroes and new leaders.

There is no conductor, no manager, just the owner. A little tipsy, he gets up to the Mic, and explains the few rules to everyone: *"Quiet down, Quiet down, Thanks fo' comin' tonight. We got an open Mic and here be the rules: Be cool an' don' step on nobody's time. Have respeck for all the great notes comin' from the stage and the people making dem notes. An'... don' throw nuthin' at the stage, 'cept monies."* He takes a big drag on his cigar, a deep slug from his drink and wanders off the stage to laughs and applause. In other words, the stage has been set to have some fun, work together and make some new music…we are all in this together. It will only work if we are. Then the first couple of people make their way to the stage, plug in, and begin an evening of discovery.

Collaboration is that *"Open Mic Blues Jam."* The old model of teamwork lacks innovation; it is like an orchestral performance. Granted, the orchestra can perform brilliantly and be moving and highly entertaining, but it has a fixed staff of players, whose performances are thoroughly pre-planned and minutely rehearsed. And you will never hear the Conductor ask the audience if there is *"…someone out there who would like to take a whack at first violin?"* The limits are defined. No one gets to explore a melody or riff off the sheet music. The participants are defined. The outcome is defined. We love orchestra because 99.9 percent of us could never come close to that level of musical talent and mastery. It has its place, its discipline and can even help some of us dream. On the other hand, you won't find too much innovation going on during or as a result of the performance. And don't even THINK of trying to participate by standing up and yelling *"You GO Brother, I feel it, I feel it!"* You'll be asked to leave.

Most organizations in business think that an orchestrated performance will lead to innovation and solutions or at least new ideas. Not.

The old model of great workplaces allowed the command and control of the orchestra analogy to reach deep into their structures. *"And the times they are a 'changin."*

In a Blues Jam, almost everyone there is convinced that they could play or sing in some manner and be part of the event.

It is, by its very nature, open to anyone who would try. The open nature and the closeness to the stage draws you in. You feel part of the proceedings. You simply feel like you can be counted and be a contributor. If you do get a shot and don't measure up, the audience will let you know if you need to step aside, or one of the players will kindly point the way back to your chair with his eyes.

The Jam relies upon a *flow of talent* wanting/ willing/ hoping to come on then off the stage, mixing new people and talents with old. Players will take chances with new riffs or lines of a song and will play off of each other's talents. This *"Jam"* (Collaboration) produces new music, new interpretations of old music…and innovations never heard before. Some memories last, some don't, but everyone involved (audience, players) come away feeling that THEY had something to do with the success of the evening (into the early mornings). They were INVOLVED.

The orchestra is an example of Command and Control, producing beautifully predictable music that we can enjoy and go home with in our heads. Few people ever describe an orchestra performance as Innovative and thought-provoking. Except perhaps a few musicians who helped script the performance. One note off the written score and the entire performance is panned as amateurish; a failed attempt to achieve what was expected.

In the Jam one hears: *"Hey Brother. C'mon up here and show us some love." "Hey Sister, ya got some sweet lines for us?" "Hey brother, I'm tired, can you take over?" "Let the brother have some."* When players get together there is no race, no age, no demand for a certain education and no true hierarchy except for talent, ideas and commitment.

Players are pushing themselves in new directions, trying out that shower-soaked riff from this morning's wake-up, or song line. The audience is reacting to the closeness and the greatness and due to that, engaging the players and the players engage the audience in new levels of discovery and adrenaline.

Eric Clapton was discovered at a blues jam in London when he was 16-years old. Jimi Hendrix mastered his craft in blues houses in Seattle, Nashville, New York and London. The best performers have always learned their trade from others through sharing, watching, exchanging and listening. And the Jam is the ultimate platform.

In a Jam…there is OPEN learning. People watching someone perform music of which they can only dream, or JUST outside their reach…today. In the Jam there are musicians complimenting each other with their instruments, facilitating each other's best talents. It is open, encouraging, engaging, reaching, touching and a fertile ground for exploration and experimentation, the drivers of innovation.

And it isn't an orchestra.

Does it work all the time? No. It takes time and INCLUSION to produce a result. Just like a collaboration.

The Take-Aways:
Collaborations need sanction. An authority figure has to endorse and set free the actual channels of the collaborative process by showing the trust necessary for all participants to play and share.

Rules (a few) need to be set. Note that the owner of the jazz club gave simple rules that were *"people"* oriented: Respect. That was it. Simple. Respect. The owner doesn't leave the premises nor will he tolerate bad behavior that disrupts the process. It's all about the positive potential that comes through by focusing on the process. Don't mess with the process.

The owner will cheerlead for the best talent. He'll get up and point at the players, buy them a drink and be supportive. He'll also encourage those who tried and failed. *"C'mon back next week an' try again. You're getting it!"*

EVERYONE is involved in some way. People will support what they help create. Remember, even the audience believes they had a hand in creating the experience.

"Give the drummer some." Give people their chance to participate and experiment, to innovate. The crowd will give them their due, be it good or not so good. Set up properly, even failure or near failure will get a round of applause for effort and guts. Especially the guts.

A Jam can be chaotic. Recognize it, embrace it, take what it gives you and deflect it back into the process, work with it. Don't try to totally control it. Chaos can breed innovation and new directions. Some people say that was how the earth and universe were created.

Collaborations happen best with both insiders and outsiders (Players and Audience in this analogy). But, collaborations are NOT exercises in teamwork. Teamwork is one group, one set of talents, as in the basketball team.

Collaborations invite disparate talents and views. Collaborations are NOT exercises in Diversity. They ARE diversity. Collaborations are open, not planned and controlled. Diversity simply happens in a collaborative effort.

The Great Workplace 2.0 ENGAGES its Participants…and encourages them to…Participate.

Jammin'

Author's note: In the late 60s, two white-looking kids (star high school athletes and performing musicians) got some fake IDs, picked up their guitar cases and went to a Blues Club near E. 55th St. in the heart of inner-city Cleveland, to experience some *"real music."* Imagine the faces of the regular patrons when we walked in. After a few minutes, everything was cool. And we DID answer their question, *"Can you play?"*

"Yeh," they said, *"dem boyz can."*

Collaboration:
The Ultimate Opportunity for Human Resources

Executive Summary:
- Human Resources typically takes on the roles of *"Keeper of the Castle"* (compliance, employee screening), *"Switchboard"* (represents the company to employees about organizational matters, benefits) and *"Exterminator"* (involved in firing).
- With Collaboration proving to be a critical factor in creating Great Workplaces, it is time for HR professionals to step up and out.

HR professionals get a horrible rap. The derisive nicknames alone are legion! Except for their own profession, no one really understands them. Most HR professionals are simply doing what every other HR pro does: Keep the castle safe, and try to make it productive. Follow the rules of the government (tear your hair out) and company (sometimes non-existent). It is an uphill fight, if not impossible, to make a true difference in the profitability of an organization when you are focused on *"protection"* duties or having anything related to *"employees"* dumped in your lap.

The real issue is that for 50+ years HR really has not changed or been able to change their focus, just the titles that describe what they do. Example: *"Personnel"* became *"Human Resources"* and now the same function is under the *"Talent Management"* or *"Workforce Management"* department.

Most HR people still do the same things: They administer benefits, hiring, training, development, rules, payroll, government paperwork, reporting and safety. They do other good things too, but nothing that to owners or *"C"* level managers makes a true difference to the bottom line of the organization, directly. The old duties will NOT plow a path to the holy grail of *"A Seat At The Table"*. Instead of *"demanding"* that SEAT, let's look at a skill that HR can develop that WILL be unique and will have the BANG the profession needs. Collaboration (NOT Teamwork):

Collaboration for Human Resources:
Collaboration is NOT Teamwork, even though the concept of *"Teamwork"* can be a component of collaborative groups. A successful team requires collaboration; a successful collaboration does not require a formal team. HR has *"Teamwork"* down cold: Get a group of people to all work together and create something good. Make sure people get along and follow the rules. Hire talent that is a lot like the talent already employed to achieve like results. Get people to salute the company flag and win one for the Gipper! Make sure everyone has the same goal(s) in mind; the company's goals. MOST people understand Teamwork, even grade-school athletic coaches.

The Great Workplace 2.0 defines **Collaboration** as: Taking disparate points of view, disparate purposes and focusing best creative talents, knowledge and attention on a single (Different) purpose, solve an issue, create something new, and go back to your own purposes. Collaboration INVITES and encourages different talents to use those talents in different ways than normal. Collaboration invites people who would not normally be Participants to a team to become intimately involved, albeit on a temporal basis.

Collaboration looks beyond the walls of an organization to *"Best Knowledge"* and *"Best Innovation"* that can be incorporated to solve issues, create opportunities and build new futures. This INVITES all Participants to become involved and to assist with their expertise in helping the organization move forward. This means that Vendors, Board members, the Community, other teams within the organization, crowd-sourced expertise and also the typically IGNORED members of the organization (*"They wouldn't understand"*) are invited/ encouraged to participate on an equal and recognized basis.

Collaboration recognizes that TALENT for problem solving or creation/ ideation does not have to come from the department or group that is suffering from the problem or the one holding the opportunity. It recognizes that different points of view (Diversity of Thought versus same-talent group assumptions) can have an enormous impact on solutions, ones that an inbred group just simply does NOT see?

Collaborations are about *"Best Thoughts"* (this goes beyond *"Best Practices"* as that term simply means what someone else has done, that worked, not what has not worked). Best Thoughts are not static, nor is Collaboration. Collaborations FLOW and change with each added thought or argued hypothesis. Best thoughts happen many times at *"Serendipity"* (thank you Jack Ricchiuto at JackZen.com). Serendipity is essentially great discoveries, by accident or ones that had an intent on another purpose. Serendipity doesn't happen in environments where the same thing, with the same people, happens all the time.

Human Resources is all about people, expertise, genesis and generating value through human resources put to work on organization goals and purposes. Collaborations are for excellence today and the next iteration of organizational excellence. In essence, Collaborations innovate, and extend the endurance of the organization forward.

To achieve that *"seat at the table"*, The way to do it is to study the Collaborative process, become expert at facilitation, and to influence and lead the organization to implement those methodologies. Collaborations get results or encourage ideation that gets results. And those bottom line results will advance HR. No other function in an organization has the foundation, skills and view that HR does. *"Line department managers"* tend to be task oriented, and Collaborations are VISIONARY. It is THE opportunity of this century for HR: Lead Collaborative efforts to affect the bottom line of any organization. No one else touches the same diversity of organizational assets as can Human Resources.

Act Local

Executive Summary:

- *"Think Global, Act Local"* is a popular business phrase today emphasizing the proposed ethical responsibilities to support their local economies and civic initiatives. Yes, buying locally will help the local economy, local taxes, local schools and if you are buying from an organization where your employees' families are employed, it could also help you.
- Acting Local goes beyond purchasing. It is engaging the community, supporting local charities and causes and contributing to local organizations, financially and intellectually.

The majority of The Great Workplaces understand that engaging the community is important and that the payback for doing so exceeds the dollars spent.

Buy Local. Yes, I can get a better price if I buy from China or out of state! This makes perfect sense if what you need can be found nowhere else. Are you certain that ABC company over in the next town won't bend over backwards to get your business or do custom work? You are a business owner, and that potential vendor has one, too. Make a phone call, take a tour, have lunch and see if Mike Jones and Company can't bring a greater and more personal value to your purchasing locally. Save shipping. Inspect locally. Have your people collaborate with theirs. Being close to a supplier may also result in learning something you want to know, or didn't even know you needed to know.

Perhaps Mike Jones buys locally from vendors you didn't even know existed. By getting to know Mike, he could be a wealth of information. And Mike may even benefit from your knowledge. Maybe you become new friends? Heck, the two of you may even get out to his/her or your club for golf or dinner. The point here is that both of you are hard at work on and in your businesses, and could mutually benefit from the relationship. His employees could, and yours could too. The Great Workplace SEEKS knowledge and collaboration outside its four walls. Entrepreneurs need to seek out other entrepreneurs and business leaders to further their own understandings.

The Great Workplaces combine two critical components to success in one: 1.) buying locally supports the community and you will get known for that; 2.) buying locally AND actively collaborating with your vendors gets you respect and knowledge. The relationship can be easier and deeper. Buying out of the region and at arm's length to actual collaboration may seem to be what the *"big guys"* do, but being a Great Workplace is all about being remarkable, not just big.

Walmart or Mom'n Pop Hardware: Yes, it does make a difference, and not just on price. Mom 'n Pop know everything about everything in their store, where it is, where it comes from and how it works. The kids at Walmart know where an isle is. When you need advice or a recommendation, Mom 'n

Pop are there. And with price-pressures to stay in business, you probably won't be taking out a loan to buy hammers. Their family has been a staple in the community for decades, and is simply asking for a chance to stay that way. If just 100 local businesses bought from the locals, there would be fewer boarded up store fronts and strip malls, and former employees moving out of town. The same holds true for Home Depot versus Mom 'n Pop. Home Depot is big, fun and they have knowledgeable people. It is your choice where your cash will go. The same holds true for your potential customers. If they could buy from you locally and you are known for buying locally, that reputation gets around. It is showing that you and your organization put some thought behind your neighbors.

Chambers of Commerce: The reputation is that most local chambers are nothing more than insurance agents selling to printers who sell to insurance agents. They are there for a reason. For them, it works. But Chamber meetings are more than just selling to members. Members help the local economy, politics, attitudes of local governing bodies about businesses in the community and with larger membership; help promote the community to other potential businesses and people who are looking to move into a geography (Potential customers and potential employees!).

But your greatest contribution to your Chamber is not your $150 per year membership and a few bucks for a pressed-chicken luncheon; it can be your opinions and your expertise. Chambers need your successes to rub off on other members and the chamber itself. You can and will make indirect and direct contributions to the success of others by discussions, networking and being on a committee. You may even meet some very interesting people. Again, potential customers, employees and influencers will be there too. And if your business runs into any speed bumps with local governing bodies, your reputation as an active member of your local Chamber will not hurt. Heck, you may even find good insurance and printing deals. If you prefer other social activities, get some of your people involved. It may expand their horizons and pride of supporting local.

Collaborative Organizations designed to Connect Local Businesses: In Northeast Ohio, we are fortunate to have MANY local organizations and Universities that have programs designed to connect local business, entrepreneurs, suppliers and buyers. Local universities and community colleges are well known for reaching out to the local business economies to Collaborate on research and practical applications, workforce development and skills training designed specifically for local workplaces, and best practices courses designed to connect local businesses with local expert knowledge. The University of Akron, Cleveland State, Case Western Reserve, Baldwin Wallace, The Ohio State University local expansion campuses, Lorain and Lakeland Community Colleges, Tri-C and Corporate College have a plethora of courses designed to support local businesses. Some even have in-house *"space for rent"* for startups and businesses that need an office and support, at reasonable rental costs.

COSE is a leading organization connecting local business with, well, just about everything. Employers Resource Council (ERC) specifically supports the HR community and organizations that do not have an onboard HR specialist. ERC provides deep resources, training and ongoing professional support to help local organizations become great places to work. They are the host organization for the prestigious NorthCoast 99 Award, Top Workplaces of Northeast Ohio. The organization is lead by Pat Perry, whom I had the pleasure of first meeting when we were both employed by AIM Executive in the early 90s. It is well-known that my company,

Champion Personnel System, Inc., is a multiple-year winner of the NorthCoast 99 award, along with Weatherhead 100 and Northeast Ohio Business Award.

Manufacturing Mart/ Capital of Know-How is a unique organization to Northeast Ohio, designed to link local manufacturing organizations with local suppliers, knowledge and expertise. Headed by connections expert Mary Kaye Denning, Manufacturing Mart provides full-cycle knowledge and supply expertise for buyers and suppliers, marketing, technology and workforce development initiatives. Their Manufacturing Expo is a good gathering place for suppliers and purchasers and is a wonderful tool in getting connected with other knowledgeable manufacturing executives.

Community Involvement: On a group plant tour with the John Carroll University Entrepreneurs Association of a Cleveland manufacturing icon (second generation ownership), I was shocked to learn just how far *"Community Involvement"* can go, and the paybacks to the organization and community. This plant facility is located in a residential and factory area of Cleveland proper. Old homes, with old factories close by are the norm. The CEO explained to us their extensive attention to their land and facilities so that the organization's property would be the *"nicest in the area."* The public and residents in the area deserved it, and it would be an example of what could be done with some care and attention. It definitely was. Residents did their best to keep up, and it showed. Nothing of the exterior was fancy, it was eco-friendly, and attractive. Inviting rather than industrial rust-belt, go-away drab. It actually looked better than some of the inside of the facility.

But here was the surprising part; on a regular basis, the community was invited to the facility for tours, refreshments and to hear speeches about the organization's environmental practices (very impressive by the way), company operations, history and future plans. Ownership and management (including the 80-year-old founder) participated, and applications for employment were respectfully taken. The organization always asked for feedback on proposed projects. When possible, local contractors were hired for work. Local politicians were invited to attend as were neighborhood groups, churches and charities. To the organization, it did not matter if five people attended or one hundred, the show went on.

The community's response? The CEO told me the organization was treated like family. Two-way respect. Never a break-in nor vandalism, nor any reason to call the authorities. A great example of Connect : Engage : Collaborate. Yes, there is an Intellectual Property gamble. Hide stuff, disguise it. It can be worth the public relations to your own people, that the Leader and the organization do in fact support your Values, Purpose and Missions.

Promote the region. The idea that *"we are all in this together"* is not only a community-used slogan, it is the truth. Many regions around the country have lost population, lost jobs, and have lost pride in their backyards. What a shame, especially in Northeast Ohio. Many of our TOP The Great Workplaces have NOT lost that pride and do a conscious job of promoting their backyards, and the people who live here.

Websites of TOP organizations either promote the region directly, bragging about the attractiveness of the region or their community and they provide links to organizations that do it for a living. Positively Cleveland regularly shows up as a regional promoter on these sites, as do the top technology innovators, government sites, park systems, links to Cleveland's professional sports teams and many more. Cleveland Plus (CLE+, also known as Positively Cleveland) is a wonderful organization promoting Cleveland/ Akron/ Northeast Ohio and is a business RESOURCE for all businesses in our Region. For full disclosure, Champion Personnel is an endorsed and preferred provider of staffing services for all conventions and business events put on with the help of Positively Cleveland at the IX Center and other facilities in our area. I would also recommend Team NEO, The Cleveland Foundation, and Greater Cleveland Partnership as exceptional resources. I am excited to say that several top executives of these organizations have been directly interviewed for this book.

TOP organizations that know they will need to relocate individuals to the area for employment also use and promote organizations like Executive Arrangements, owned by Margy Judd. Since 1978 Executive Arrangements has been the trusted advisor to hundreds of corporations and organizations in Northeast Ohio who want assistance in introducing potential newcomers to our region in Northeast Ohio. The staff of Executive Arrangements is composed of long-term residents of the area, highly engaged in the community and experts on anything potential newcomers may want to know. Unlike many people who are motivated by selling a home, this staff is motivated by Connecting and Engaging their clientele in their total relocation concerns and experience. Their success rate is off the charts. Margy has been a long-term member and past Chair of the John Carroll Entrepreneurs Association (JCUEA keeps coming up, doesn't it), and one of the most enthusiastic entrepreneurs in the region herself.

The top Great Workplaces take the time to look locally, support their communities, and participate in local initiatives, even when they have to buy some items from overseas due to pure cost. But they look local first. It simply supports their reputation in the area. The Great Workplace knows that their Participants, for the most part, are local, and are looking to see how their *"employer"* supports the communities and businesses where they live.

Acting Local is Tribal in nature, here represented by our Great Workplaces analogy of the Tipi as the organization versus the typical 2-D rendering of a pyramid (please see our explanation of the Tipi). "Tribal" in this sense of the term means *"Shared Purpose or Purposes,"* where the Purpose entails egalitarian (everyone being equal and important) values. What is good for the organization is good for the community, and vice versa. One supports the other, but neither attracts the other until action to do so takes place in an observable way. As actions take place in a continual manner, they produce a mutual support and kinship. In other words, it is up to you to take the first step.

Intelligently Profitable

Executive Summary:
- Profit is good. Remarkable Organizations do have solid track records when it comes to their bottom lines.
- The most Remarkable Organizations practice Intelligent Profitability as a component of their endurance (Organization Sustainability). This is a qualitative focus that reflects Values, Purpose and Intelligent Self Interest for all Participants.

All measures of business success dictate that profitability on a consistent basis is the only way to operate an organization. In our current economy the words *"Profit"* and *"Consistent"* together may sound like an urban legend. The breeze off the wings of butterflies in Germany may seem to have more affect on your bottom line than your best strategic plans.

So when the Top Great Workplaces are profitable, what do they do? They act like squirrels! They salt away a sufficient amount of cash according to sound predictions so as to not have to frantically search for nuts during the winter. That should be obvious to anyone.

Then they Invest. In themselves.

Certainly they invest in equipment, software, facilities and infrastructure that support their growth and future. They fix stuff, upgrade stuff and mow the lawn. Whereas the most Remarkable Organizations take additional strategic moves:

1) They invest in their people. Training, schools, additional contributions to 401Ks, small company gatherings to promote teamwork and Culture, and *"awards"* for Collaborations, team performances and innovations. The Best realize that during tight times, the Passion of the TEAM and the individuals can get rocked. The organization's Values can get put aside during survival drills and raises could be curtailed due to uncertainties. The top Great Workplaces know that it really is not the money in the award, it is the recognition and the affirmation of jobs and efforts well done that motivates participants. Training, development, recognitions, group gatherings and work environment improvements are Single Events. They are not necessarily fixed, ongoing expenses.

2) They invest in functional upgrades. Yes, that even means separations of people who are not long-term, future contributors, and the acquisition of new Right People who will be. Top organizations during tough times see exactly who the winners are, keep them and begin to look for solutions to business issues by bringing in new talent. This is building Endurance into the foundation of the organization. During the troubled times it is easy to *"lay off"* underperforming people. The TEAM will think

that is the easy method of extraction. When done during good times, the TEAM gets a different message: the organization is serious about improving OUR future.

3) Top Organizations invest in community-building activities. Investing is not just money; it is sharing of guidance and time. Investing in your community is a *"How"* of developing a Great Workplace. It is investing in goodwill, Connecting with the community in which you live and operate and it is just the Right thing to do. Top Great Workplaces have always found that it is a payback activity in public opinion, talent search and brand building, even if your product is not bought by the community. It lets your own staff know that your Values are real.

4) Remarkable Organizations feed their engines of Innovation. They invest in, *"What if we could _____?"* And use their assets to more deeply communicate with customers and potential customers. They take the opportunity of Profit and turn it into time spent on Customer Purpose delivered or improvements to be made. *"Business as usual"* is not their mantra.

5) Using the methodology of David Cooperrider's (Case Western Reserve University. http://appreciativeinquiry. case.edu/intro/whatisai.cfm) Appreciative Inquiry (*"What are we doing extremely well?"*), Remarkable Organizations seek out their own strengths, refine them or expand those differentiators. They will look for issues of course, but knowing what (How) works, they seek to capitalize on it. It may seem counter-intuitive to spend time further refining or innovating something that isn't broken, but that is human nature talking, not strategic thinking. Anything worth doing well is worth over-doing well.

6) Top leaders resist paying themselves big bonuses and stuffing the money into luxury cars or off-shore accounts that cannot be accessed for the good of the organization in the future. There will be a time for that, when you cannot think of any profitable project for the organization. People who paid themselves first in the past are the ones driving the 12-year old Mercedes S class in need of repairs.

7) Remarkable Organizations do simple things like painting, cleaning and organizing their environments to provide a more friendly and productive place for all participants, right down to the 20-year old peeling paint job in the visitor's lobby.

8) Remarkable Organizations invest in Green Technology or similar forward-thinking efficiencies. The time will never be perfect, but they do it as a future investment and it is the right thing to do.

Remarkable Organizations practice Intelligent Profitability by strategic thinking and actions. It is much easier for a privately held (non-stock) organization to do so than a public company where shareholders need to see an EPS that out-performs analyst's expectations. Private owners know that increasing the value of their own investment and building a Great(er) Workplace will create a better future for all Participants. It will give the organization more flexibility and foundation to focus on their Purpose, Values and productive Culture, which will create new and more satisfied Customers.

Here is the way to start:

1) You have made a decent profit. How much do you need for ongoing operations? What is left?

2) Look at the eight items above that Intelligently Profitable, Remarkable Organizations think about and act on.

3) Make a *"Mission"* for the ones you will act on, or Innovate from those ideas. Relate each Mission to your Purpose, Values and Culture. Allocate your funds accordingly.

4) Smile. You just improved your future net worth without impressing your neighbors with a *"Shiny New Thing"* parked in your driveway. Perhaps you can do both and have that smile 24/7.

5) If after you invest in your Missions, and still have money left over, send some to me. We'll both feel better.

Visible Tangible Leadership

Executive Summary:

- You took on the role of owner or high-level manager for your own motivations. With that as a foundation, you have an "Image" of whom you want to be, what you want to project to your staff or body of participants.
- Take this litmus test: Does your entire persona Connect, Engage and Collaborate with the people you intend to influence, or are you simply trying to justify that image you created?
- Are you achieving the organizational and personal RESULTS you envisioned? Have you developed a core of Purpose-driven principles and values that will not be shaken or used only as poster fodder in your (fancy) lobby? Think hard and honestly about this, then read on.

Observing hundreds of CEOs/ Owners and Management-level people in Great and not-so-great workplaces, one hard truth surfaces about Leadership: It is a cause-and-effect relationship that must be evaluated, tweaked, learned and lived with. It is RARE that a CEO simply has been *"born"* to be an effective leader of people, ideas and collaborative results. Leaders have to work HARD at being effective. Leadership as a concept in today's business world is anything but a casual exercise in projecting oneself into a business environment.

Leadership, by necessity, is developed through having a constant Sonar-like feedback system of how you are affecting not only people, but also your systems and plans, and those Participants to the success of your organization with whom you may not consistently interact. Much of that feedback system is internal (reflection and analysis), that is fed by external sources; noticing how you affect results, people, management and growth. A true leader has a high degree of self-awareness.

External feedback comes from management, fearless participants (employees, board, vendors, customers), and consultants and of course the ever-important fiscal/ growth chart (financial statement, and other scoreboards). Your feedback system should be *"constantly on"* like sonar. It will tell you where you are going, and how you are doing. Frankly, it is not only your job, but your duty to yourself, family, organization and your combined futures. And it should be what drives you.

If the essence of Who you are, the image you are trying to project, is working (results), and people are prone to following you, and they feel and ACT like they are connected and engaged with your projection of not only the organization you are creating, but you as the mirror of all that, you are doing quite well. Keep it up but, *"stay thirsty my friend."* The economy and marketplace are not stagnant and the needs of your participants will continually ebb and flow. As a naturally effective leader, you are one of the few (1 percent). Great leaders are constantly learning, about everything as a matter of fact, but they are learning what affect they have on end results.

By definition, a leader has followers. He or she has built a team. In some cases those followers can be forced zombie-like and are totally guided by a single word uttered by their leader. That method has a short shelf-life, and may only be good for weekend inventory counts. It is however, amazing how many owners believe in this leadership image. It only lasts as long as the leader can keep playing that role. And its true effectiveness is doubtful. Many potential leaders default to a dictatorial style, which may be good or bad depending upon circumstances. It is well known that people in influential positions have this as a tendency, albeit not well thought-through. When you default to being a dictator, know that people may eventually forget what you have said, but they will never forget how you made them feel.

A true leader earns fully aware and engaged followers, who share a vision and multiple purposes, are collaborators to the purpose and vision, embrace the values represented by the leader and who feel motivated to be led. It is their choice to make, not yours.

Here Are A Few Simple Questions To Ask Yourself About Your Leadership Effectiveness:

1) When you walk around your organization, do people look DIRECTLY at you, or do they avoid eye contact? Do you look directly at them? It is NOT necessary that people stop productive activities to catch your glance, but when they could, do they?

2) Do your people look and act Engaged in their activities? Engaged means they are purposeful, energetic and focused in their tasks. Are those people smiling in a way that shows willful pleasure in what they are doing? Are they engaged in conversations and activities that continue when you pass, or do they flee to another physical space? If they do, that shows more of wasting

time than engaging in productive work or conversations. Will an outsider visiting your facility feel the same about what he/she sees, hears and feels?

3) Do you hear your organization's Values, Purpose and Missions being used in conversations between your staff, customers, vendors, and to potential recruits? Do these people recant stories of victories earned through the purposeful application of your Values, Purpose and the Principles for which you stand?

As you walk within your organization, what you, another manager or an outsider will see, hear and feel is the organization's tangible Culture. And Culture is defined as Values in Action. It is the NOW of what you have built, good or not-so-good. Culture can be considered the end product of organizational leadership. It is a reflection of the leadership given to the *"Tribe"* of your organization.

Because I often work as a consultant with my clients, I have the opportunity to walk through hundreds of facilities. The evident Culture of an organization is tangible, even in a quiet, laboratory-like facility. It is evident on faces, in the pace of movement, in the focus of eyes and in the general posture of all people. But like anything, that first impression is not always accurate to the casual observer. One can get fooled, but not often. Culture is evident, so is lack of Culture.

Know that people today want and need leadership, even though they may talk and act to the contrary. Today's cautious attitude toward employment and frequent job-changing is more due to lack of leadership and solid management than any other factor. That is exactly where good, tangible and visible leadership is an organizational return on investment (ROI): Leadership shows and confirms Purpose, promotes the Values, and Shares the future vision. Leadership attracts and keeps The Right People, motivates them to do The Right Things, and focuses those people to do the Right Things, Right; consistently, and with purpose.

Is Leadership a style? It is, and it is not. My close friend, mentor and associate David Akers, founder and CEO of Collaborent Group Ltd. (Collaborent Group is a unique organization. It is a management company that designs, implements and operates collaborative business models for groups of organizations to control costs and improve operations). David uses a great analogy: *"Effective leaders are like great athletes: they come in different sizes, shapes and methods of winning. Each has his/her own way of getting to the scoreboard. But they all get there. Great athletes are involved in different games and need to approach those challenges according to the challenge."*

I have met with every conceivable personality of company owner, C-level executive and Human Resource executive. Many are self-styled commando-like monsters. Many are judgmental of participants (Vendors included), and many are so darn afraid of being taken advantage of they come across as freezer-cold or arrogant.

Then there are the Learned Leaders of Great Workplaces. Some are not the founders or owners, but they are the *"Leader with Credentials"* and they are remarkable people. Many of those have very smart CEOs who know they themselves are better kept in an office and have sanctioned high-level subordinates to fill the role of organizational leadership. They have trained and educated their own Command Staff to carry the torches. But first, they hired The Right People to do so.

As mentioned in another chapter, in a previous life I worked for Capital American Insurance as a Division VP, met and talked with the owner/Chair Barry Hershey. Barry lived in

Boston, taught at Harvard, and as a result was an absent owner. But Barry was very smart, and had other *"leaders with credentials:"* David Lazar, President, who had been the CFO of Progressive Insurance; Tom Bresnan, Division President then Corporate President; Board Member Richard Osborne, Dean Emeritus of Case Western Reserve University School of Business; and vic gelb (sic — spelled the way he does) an entrepreneur/philanthropist of the highest degree in Northeast Ohio.

These four gentlemen had different personalities: Lazar, intellectual and insightful. Bresnan, hard-charging and dynamic. Osborne, elegant, charismatic and slightly eccentric (known affectionately to his students as *"The Gorilla"*). gelb, focused, challenging and direct. vic could pierce into your soul. But each carried an identical message about the organization, the future and expectations of their reports. They visibly, tangibly, held the corporate Values, Mission, Purpose and Culture in their every word. There was never a doubt what was expected of any participant and that the Vision was the mission each and every day. It was an honor to be with them. Each one of them asked (constantly) *"What do you think?"* And stood square-shouldered to you, intently listening to your answer. You not only felt important, but accountable, even if they disagreed with you. And when that happened, their response guided and developed you for the future. There were many *"Ah-Hah"* moments with these gentlemen.

The result of their leadership? In the four years I spent with Capital American, the company grew astronomically, and was eventually sold to Canseco for about a half a billion dollars.

Leaders create culture. We define culture as *"Values in Action."* Lobby signs and newsletter banners can't effectively achieve culture. Those signs and banners become targets of jokes when they are not manifestly visible and tangible by top management or subordinate leaders.

In a recent discussion with Ron Weinberg, enormously successful builder and former Chair/CEO of the HAWK Corporation (the company was sold in 2011), I pointedly asked Ron how he was able to build the successful culture at HAWK. His response was quick and to the point: *"You talk about values at every opportunity, and we celebrated successes of our core values at every opportunity."* One of HAWK's core values is that Winning (Work) is Fun, and achievements are recognized. To Ron, achievements that reflect core values are a way to visibly and tangibly remind everyone that the core values are more than signs on a wall. They are real, make a difference, and are the foundation to success of the organization and individual/ team participants. By repeating these core values, showing HOW they play a central focus to the success of the organization and its participants, these Values become tangible. The Leader becomes the mirror of those values. The true Leader lives the Values, becomes tangible visible and iconic. The Values, Purpose, Missions, Culture AND the Leadership become remarkable.

The result at HAWK? The organization was built from humble beginnings ($8 mil) and sold for over $400 million.

In one of the top Great Workplaces, the owner/founder can frequently be found on the shop floor dressed in a company work shirt. He is NOT wandering around. He is engaged in meaningful conversations and inquiries with shop floor participants and supervisors. There is intensity to these meet-ups. The founder is totally present and focused on the person and conversation. He is not there for show. He is inquiring about projects, production, issues and is constantly a reminder of the organization's core values, purpose for the customer and the organization's goals and missions. He is totally engaged and involved; talk about dressed for success! This owner asks the most valuable question that can be asked today: *"What do YOU think?"* That question connects, engages and begs for collaboration from anyone who is asked. It makes the person receiving the question feel of value. It motivates and energizes Innovation, reduces the fear of being inconsequential and demands thoughtful, supportable answers.

This owner has a regular, conversational column in the organization's newsletter. His articles always reflect Values and Purpose and are both congratulatory and directive in nature. He appears in company product, history and technology videos, most of which give the impression that there is no script, with the founder speaking from his heart and head. The viewer is positive the founder is speaking directly to him or her, not an audience. The founder is a Leader, engaged, and visibly tangible.

Some leadership styles and applications can be both simple and extraordinarily effective. In the early 1980's I was privileged (by marriage) to have an *"inside view"* at Johnson Rubber and Plastics Company in Middlefield, Ohio. Grandpa Miller, the almost retired, long-term owner/ CEO of, at the time, a highly successful company, handed out every paycheck personally to every shop-floor employee and thanked them for their great work. He knew every person's name, their kids' names and something unique about each person. Friendly, personal and high-touch, Grandpa was also relentless in the boardroom, in business meetings and in standing up for the principles he valued as a leader of people; and the man who had the ultimate accountability for jobs, families, vendors and customers.

And that was not the amazing part. The Human Resource Director showed me a list of all employees at the Middlefield facility, single-spaced with their years of employment next to their names. I turned 20 pages until the list showed employment UNDER 20 YEARS! Yes, it was the 1980s. Yes it was Middlefield, not urban Cleveland, Columbus or Chicago. But there were countless other companies within driving distance to that facility, and Johnson's employees were NOT paid better than all of the rest.

One of Grandpa Miller's prize possessions was an aerial photo of the facility and the parking lot hung on a wall outside his office. The photo was at least 20-years old at the time. It showed many cars, but also showed clearly one third of the parking spaces were taken up by horse buggies of local Amish who worked there. I made a note to see if that was the same on that day. It had dwindled down to about 20 percent. Not due to fewer Amish, simply more non-Amish employees and a larger parking lot. And one thing I know being a long-time Geauga County resident; if you lie or try to fool an Amish worker, they will all walk on you and not look back. Grandpa built trust. Grandpa built a company on values, connection and engagement, and *"touch."*

The result? The company continued to grow and provided great careers to over 1,000 people. The main company spun off a new division (with a little help from me and my recruiting company) named Johnsonite, which became a world leader in their products and was purchased by a European concern. The remaining Johnson companies were spun off to family members (successfully). Unfortunately, Johnson Rubber came to an unfortunate halt in the late 1990s. Champion Personnel had a bitter-sweet assignment to provide workers to help close the facility. Grandpa Miller remained in the hearts of many of the exiting workers. I will leave the story there.

Passion and Vision. Do they matter? As long as the core values, purpose and missions the Leader promotes are at the center of that Passionate Vision. A friend and business Mentor is Ray Dalton of PartsSource Inc. Ray has received too many achievement awards to faithfully mention each here, but *"Ernst and Young Entrepreneur Of The Year"* should be a good foundation. Awards include Civic, Customer Service, Non Profit, Innovations, Employee Environment, Supply Chain Management, Employee Growth and many more. Ray and I met at our mutual first Weatherhead 100 Award Ceremony. PartsSource was #1, Champion was #50.

Ray has founded and sold at least seven successful organizations. He is an author, *"Proceed with Confidence. Lessons learned from a Serial Entrepreneur"* (New Vista Partners, available on Amazon), which is about the person, values learned and obstacles overcome. It is directly about becoming a leader, leadership and core values. Ray is an evangelist. Both in his faith and his visions for organizations and people.

Ray Dalton is charming, humble, grateful and captivating. He takes hard work for granted and focuses on the future Purpose, for Customers, and anyone willing to come along for the ride. His energy and Passion are not only Tangible but viral. Walk into PartsSource at anytime, and you can feel, see and hear the Culture. It is about today, but it is firmly planted in the future.

Ray's leadership is about Integrity. He promotes what he believes, and lives it. His persona invites you to reach higher, share common values and visions, and to walk the talk. He is in fact a Crusader.

The result? PartsSource is a perennial award winning organization, as is Ray as a person. They have brought in investors, made employees millionaires and continued to acquire organizations to further grow the vision. The corporate website shows every corporate employee and purposefully honors those who are Veterans of our Military Services. I have not seen another Northeast Ohio company that does that, and PartsSource has done that since its inception.

As a philanthropic person, Ray has invested his time, and personal resources to further health care in third world countries and in our own country. He does this selflessly, passionately and with joy.

Ray connects with people and participants including the community, Engages them in the Purpose and Vision of the organization, and Collaborates to achieve the success of everyone involved. At PartsSource, *"The Answer is YES"*. The customer's need is their purpose and mission. Compare that to many organizations and people today where the answer is *"Maybe, if I can get around to it."*

The characteristics I have found in true leaders can be found in my conversations with David Akers of Collaborent Ltd., who is a member of a unique group of entrepreneurs and civic leaders called **MasterMind** (the group of seven has or is serving on the boards of over 30 organizations in Northeast Ohio, owns or have launched dozens of corporate and civic organizations, have authored and are in the process of authoring numerous books, are public speakers, consultants and are voracious *"learners"*).

When David and I discussed the characteristics of *"Leaders"* our findings could not have been more in tune. Some quotes from David Akers (I have left out the " " 's for the sake of your eyesight):

- Leaders act from Principles. Principles are forged from values and become what one will stand up for when pushed to the limit.

- Leaders are not measured on their potential. Your *"limitless potential"* was built up through high school graduation. Leaders are then measured by their results.
- Leaders are truly measured on how they respond to events, both good and bad. A true leader comes through and is built by the crucible of accountability in their leadership role. How do they react? What have they learned, and what have they taken action on?
- Leaders are self-aware. They work hard at leadership. They improve; some read, some learn by asking questions, some observe. But they KNOW their own talents and leverage them.
- Leaders know where their limitations are, and *"mobilize others"* to lead certain components of the charge. They form GREAT teams by attracting and engaging talented people. These teams are built around Purpose.
- They set the bar high for themselves and others. After all, if winning isn't important in a venture, why keep score?
- The true leader has Persistence. They read and react, learn and pursue. They ultimately figure it out.
- True Leaders are never satisfied. They are driven. They tinker. They change, but they never change their values.

Like our revered Special Forces, they know that: *"The only easy day was yesterday."* To take this a step further and quote from the Navy SEAL ethos:

In times of war or uncertainty there is a special breed of warrior ready to answer our Nation's call. A common man with uncommon desire to succeed. Forged by adversity, he stands alongside America's finest special operations forces to serve his country, the American people, and protect their way of life. I am that man. I will not fail. If knocked down, I will get back up, every time. I will draw on every remaining ounce of strength to protect my teammates and to accomplish our mission. I am never out of the fight.

Just substitute the words *"TEAM"* or *"Organization"* and *"Purpose"* for the words written for these best-of-the-best warriors.

GREAT leaders find the balance in their lives between Business, Personal, Family and Faith. They know that stretched to the limit in any one direction can lead to failings in the others. A Leader is a whole person, aware and passionate about everything life has to offer.

Leadership has the 4 *"P's"*: Purpose, Persistence, Principles and Passion. The lack of any one of these makes the Leader incomplete.

To Finish Thoughts From My Findings:

True leaders don't hide in offices. They connect, engage and collaborate with their crew. They are the first to get to a customer and first to take responsibility for and action on any mistake made by their organization. They are seen and heard and are constantly reflecting Purpose, Vales and Principles. When I had just bought Champion Personnel from my father, and our long-term bookkeeper had retired, our new bookkeeper sent out an entire payroll of checks to our Interim workers, unsigned, un-signature stamped. Immediately our staff contacted each one and I spent an entire day personally going to each location, apologizing to each worker for the error and handing that person a new, personally signed check. Over the next several months we received more candidate referrals than in the year before, and our sales went sky-high. Our customers noticed, our staff noticed and our Interim workers noticed the action, not just the words.

True Leaders are the 1 percent in the mix of those with authority and intentions. They have willingly taken the burden that being in front demands. They live their Purpose and Passions; they learn and never stop learning. They don't quit. They take action when others want to discuss or pontificate.

They have built networks of support, but know that the accountability stops with them and no one else.

They are *"Champions who fight for another's honor."* They want the ball. They want results. They own their results.

Personality is not a be-all factor in leadership, unless personality is defined in terms of the four *"P's."*

Where a leader begins to fail is when they begin to read and believe their own press clippings.

Remarkable!

Transparent Integrity

Executive Summary:
- This is not only about you, the owner or manager, but about your organization and your people.
- You either have the Values of Integrity, or you don't.

To understand the concept of Transparent Integrity in organizations, let me draw an analogy with the characters of The Wizard of Oz. The Wizard put on a public face that suited his mission, in his mind. It was not the real Wizard. Dorothy had a Purpose (and subordinate mission) to return home, but used Intelligent Self Interest and a well-founded, uncontrived ethos in her journey to accomplish her purpose: she was open and transparent in her motivations, constantly and rightfully denied what doubters assumed were less heroic motivations, and while needing others to help in her journey, never sublimated nor contrived their interests for hers or hers for theirs.

Her companions were put to tests to support their true motivations while in some measure those tests were also a test of Dorothy. Dorothy was not only open about her purpose and mission, but engaged others in it. Dorothy's Purpose stood the test of sarcastic scrutiny.

Now, the Wizard; eventually his curtain is pulled aside by a neutral character; Toto. His reality was revealed for all to see. And it was not what he had made people believe. It lacked Integrity, even though he justified it in his mind, and then publically. Pulling the curtain made his true Values transparent.

Over the course of the last few decades, the value structure within a fundamental business operating plan changed from the assumption of integrity in all *"Participant"* dealings (employees, vendors, customers, board, community) to *"We need to have a Public Face (conjured set of values) to keep stakeholders or customers happy"*.

Much of the *"public versus private face"* logic was due in part to and covered by the assumption that any endeavor the company embarked upon was prey to the competition. It could be turned, twisted and re-publicized as a weakness or as a point of comparison used in marketing between the two organizations, and where one company lacked a true competitive edge, they could make one up or twist a competitor's positive into a negative.

Still more of the shift was due to an assumption that the end customer and other participants would understand convenient, end-justifies-the-means thinking. After all, the Stake Holders (old term) were really only interested in the end results, not the process.

And, in many privately held or closely held companies, the *"Chief"* is afraid to show any personal weaknesses or corporate weaknesses. Doing that could reduce the desired projected image of the organization or diminish the Chief's desired personal power with all participants. We do in fact equate the strength of a company with the persona of the CEO or other public figure of an organization. Sometimes the public is not very bright, but nevertheless, astute.

Recently, the *"public face"* has been invoked frequently to protect short term stock prices, competitive advantage, and liabilities.

Although transparency is not an exercise in revealing true competitive secrets, many organizations have taken non-transparency as a blanket rule for all that characterizes the organization and have preferred NOT to make the distinction between core integrity (a reflection of those values the organization has put forward as their Ethos) and core secrets (products, pipelines, customers, vendors, processes). The two areas of visible are not at all the same. Remarkable Organizations know the difference.

Owners, Managers, Staff, Board, Vendors and Contractors (Participants) need to have and show Integrity. And it has to be Visible. No *"two faces"*. The organization and all participants need to prove the statement (really it is a question): *"Trust me."* Trust is earned through actions, not statements encased on a wall.

Integrity (*Transparent*) needs to be a part of all core Values, and especially you the Owner need to live those Values. Your employees need to live those Values. If not, your house of cards will come falling down, quickly, more quickly today than even two-years ago. If you lack actions that reflect your stated Values, social media will nail you, hard.

An organization's Culture will show the difference in Values Acted upon versus stated Values. The same with the Owner, and your Managers, your public contact people and your outside representatives.

Culture is defined as *"Values in Action."*

Remarkable Organizations keep their Actions in line with their Values, from the bottom up. They expect it, train it, develop it and check for it. Remarkable Organizations ask their customers and their Vendors how the organization is delivering on the Purposes (Promises) and track any anomaly. When the anomaly is found, it is corrected or retrained. It is not let alone on the chance it was a simple *"error"* of process or *"human error"* of judgment (Values learned should be the guiding ethos for Judgment).

To keep this entire concept of Integrity and Transparency simple: Leaders and Participants of Remarkable Organizations are consistently acting with Integrity. They don't have to worry about Transparency. They not only reflect the Values of their organizations, they demand and expect others to do so. It is their Culture.

They *"Say what they do, do what they say, and prove it."*

Without naming people, it has been my pleasure to meet with, talk off the record with, and share experiences with some of the finest CEOs, Owners and Managers of all sizes and types of organizations, not just in Northeast Ohio, but around the country. These Great Leaders live their organization's Values, to the letter. As do their Participants.

Then there are those, who like The Wizard mentioned earlier, do not. They are NOT in charge at Remarkable Organizations.

To become a Remarkable Organization and the Leader who reflects those characteristics:

First: work on assuring that the 12 other attributes of being a Great Workplace are solid: Purpose being THE starting point. Then make sure the Purpose is reflected in your Values

(Ethos). Both Purpose and Values answer the *"Why?"* your organization exists, beyond making money, for you or your Participants. The Leader(s) need to live that way. Your Culture (*Values in Action*) will follow.

When you have the *"Why"* nailed and the *"Purpose"* to drive your direction, almost anything can be accomplished. And you will sleep better.

The Integrity part of the equation comes from doing in reality, what your Purpose (Values and Mission) say that you will do. You and each of your Participants need to reflect those values in your actions. And…especially the owner in his or her *"private"* actions. For a Leader, your private actions are sure to take a public stand, at some point, and it will come at the most awkward time.

What do you do when a Participant acts contrary to your Values? The first time may be a mistake; the second time is a choice. If you let it go to a third time, it has become a habit. Let those with contrary choices or habits become the problems of another organization. That is exactly what Remarkable Organizations do, but they rarely have to. Their Immersion, Values and Performance Management systems breed out *"mistakes"* and *"Choices"* before they become *"Habits"*.

And yes, it is okay to have a *"Mission"* as long as you understand that is has a time frame, is totally self-centered and is not a substitute for Purpose.

The Enduring Organization

Executive Summary:
- The Enduring Organization is the result of implementing all 13 characteristics of The Great Workplace. It is the culmination of nurturing Values, Purpose, and strategy from within an Integrated Operating Plan.
- It moves the organization away from hopes and wishes as strategies and firmly plants it as an icon to customers and participants.
- Enduring is principle-based and encompasses the Why, the How, and the What of the organization's offerings.
- The components of Endurance are built, with Purpose, to be fluid enough to move with the winds of marketplace change, yet solid enough to maintain its core.

The Chinese honored their Emperor with *"10,000 Years"* of conceptual existence. The Japanese built organizations and concepts, for *"1,000 Years,"* not for this quarter's share price. Agree with the concepts as applied, the nation's politics, or not, the philosophy is solid and has been mimicked the world over. The analogy is simple: Build it to last forever and beyond. It brings confidence to the anointed organization, and the people who serve it.

When you are a business owner, it is difficult to sleep well if you do not have a firm foundation for the success of that business. During a fiscal period when all the wheels seem to be coming off, you want to re-invent everything having to do with the *"What"*, *"How"*, and especially the *"Why"* of your business, to confront and solve issues: The Sales Department is lazy. The shop manager doesn't see the bottlenecks. The sales literature was designed by a teenager. And customers just don't get it. *"I need to re-invent the company, but didn't I do that last month?"* We business owners have a predilection toward *"begin, try, burn, rebuild, and try again and again"*.

During periods of success, we become light-hearted and certain that the Gods are paying us back for all the hard work and missed home-dinners and forgotten soccer matches. We enjoy the ride; *"Don't change anything. It's all coming together, finally!"* We sleep better and our strides are confident again. Then, we get hit with another broken wheel, especially when it comes to people, their commitments and their behaviors. And we start the same emotional/ justification process all over again.

Chances are you have spent more time on the products and services and less on organizational design and the business foundation. We will call the products and services the *"What"*, and the *"How"* is the uniqueness in your *"What"*.

The smaller the organization in numbers of participants, the closer the owner is to the What and the How. The owner could be the chief sales rep or product designer and customer service rep. That owner might have a Vision for the future of the organization, and it is wrapped up in the What and the How, by necessity, or so it seems to the owner. The fact is the owner is still approaching the business not as an entity, but as a job. He or she is working *"In"* the business, not *"on"* the business. And that is a common question from advisors and from weekend speakers at seminars: *"Are you working ON or IN the business?"* *"Are you creating a vehicle for the future of your organization, or just working on the stereo system?"* Great questions, regardless of which one completes the visual for you.

An example from my search for The Great Workplaces: I spent considerable time on the phone with one organization's owner before our personal meeting and filming our in-depth session in our video studio. His presentation of the organization and their Purpose (why) was very exciting. His What and How were dead-on-target for his audience. I would have guessed he had 30-50 employees, all wearing the corporate sweater. In my personal meeting he informed me that his staff had grown from himself to 5 employees! That was in 2005. In 2012, he now has over 30 (he is in a service-oriented profession). From the beginning he had more than the What and the How. He had a true *"Why"* and constructed his business plan around it.

Every business hits some roadblocks and detours. The TOP Great Workplaces seem to experience fewer surprises that *"rock the Tipi"* and those surprises are managed within the foundational structure. The Great Workplaces have plans, principles and values that act like gyroscopes to keep the business centered. This is especially handy when owners get too emotionally involved with short-term outcomes. We all have that tendency.

After all, if the concept of an organization is good enough for the foreseeable future, why should it not endure beyond that original vision? Foundations should last beyond a current tactic and from those tactics should be bred new concepts and new results according to the new needs of the day and future.

Most organizations are built around products, services or solutions (the things we sell) that are meant to be applied in today's market, and when the target *"market need"* moves or evaporates the foundation of the organization tends to follow. In that is the rub: Profit today, scramble tomorrow, re-invent the organization around another product to survive. ALL businesses in today's market will need to re-tool according to the changes in their target-market, but how can an organization not be blown about in the wind? And after over 30 years in the business marketplace, I can testify that today's quick market movements in our global economy are nastier than ever before.

The aspirin for all this is to build your organization around Values, Purpose, the future of the Right People, and the WHY, while you are refining the What and the How. Doing so creates a foundation on which you can focus on your market niche as you refine market strategies.

In the November 2011 article *"Institutional Logic"* in the Harvard Business Review Elizabeth Moss Kanter (Director of Harvard's Advance Leadership Initiative) with the global consulting firm Oliver Wyman argued, "the value that a company creates should not be measured in terms of short-term profits or paychecks but also how **it sustains the conditions that allow it to flourish over time. These (best) corporate leaders deliver more than just financial results; they also build enduring institutions.** " (Italics and emphasis added)

How well an organization arranges their foundation (conditions) will determine their longevity. The TOP Great Workplaces have a few critical characteristics in common that achieve that Enduring quality, and with that they have been able to achieve **Remarkable** status:

1) Purpose
2) Values
3) Integrated (Collaborative) Operating Plan
4) The Right People Doing The Right Things, Right
5) Transparent Integrity with Visible, Tangible Leadership

Each of these characteristics is covered in its own chapter, but let's put them together in relationship to the Enduring Organization.

For the sake of simplicity, extract any of these characteristics from any organization and what will you get? A weak organization that will more than likely flap in the winds of change. Or if you are more animal-oriented visually, a dog chasing its own tail.

Extract **Purpose** and you will get a group of people who have no single theme from which to make decisions for the organization, and for the customer, except perhaps the Mission theme that is intrinsically motivated (short-term goal-orientation) for the organization itself. That alone, for short-term movement, may be sufficient to achieve goals, but when that theme has reached a conclusion, the game starts all over with a new one. No long-term framework and no true consideration of the customer. The *"why we exist"* is gone. The glue has dried. The customer yawns and goes elsewhere.

Extract **Values** and the organization will have no fundamental guiding principles for daily operations. As long as something in daily operations works or a method is accepted, then everything is okay. If it doesn't work today, then it must be bad. Lacking values, any behavior is acceptable. Lacking values, work becomes whatever the day's agenda happens to be. Lacking Values or Purpose, there is no platform for true collaboration. Collaboration is only effective when Shared Purpose AND Shared Values exist and are evident.

Extract the **Right People Doing the Right Things Right** and you will have *"convenient employees and management"*, vendors and other participants brought to the table with expectations of achieving results that are average at best. Even with a strong Value system and Purpose, the organization will have a tendency to mismatch talent to performance objectives, or no true performance objectives can be realistically set and met. The organization may in fact survive, profitably, but turnover will still be costly (and constant) and when push comes to shove and the winds of change blow, people who could cut it when *"average"* is the expected norm, will begin to show signs of wear.

Extract **The Integrated (and Collaborative) Operating Plan** and you will have a myriad of units functioning according to their own self-serving vision, even if a unit or two look like they are on the right path. The Integrated Operating Plan is described as **"Collective Intelligence"** and should be viewed as a Tool for every participant and operating unit. In another chapter, I described the Plan as *"Poles in a Tipi"* where each individual operating unit has its own specific **What** and **How**, but they all meet at the top where the **Why** is not only the intersection, but the collar that holds them all together. The **Why** is in your **Purpose**, the reason (beyond money) your organization exists in the first place.

Extract **Visible Tangible Leadership with Transparent Integrity** and no one will know if the Wizards behind the curtain are real and support the advertised Purpose, Missions, Goals, Values and future of the organization. The **Culture** (Values in action) of the organization will disintegrate into, *"they talk a good game, but bat like St. Louis..."* or *"whatever you hear, don't believe it"* at the coffee station. At that stage of failure, it will take a complete change of management (or ownership) to reset the Tipi. Doable for sure, but expensive and time-consuming. The worst of all that is: 1) Your customers find out you cannot be trusted, and 2) Your direct competitors smell the blood in the water, and will help your customers to believe that you can't be trusted.

The **Leader** of the organization not only needs to set the tone for all to hear and see in the **How** and **Why**, that **Leader** needs to be **Visible, Tangible and exude Transparent Integrity**. People buy the **How** (differentiator) and the **Why** (your purpose directed at them). The **What** you do is mostly the same from organization to organization in the same industry (yes, it really is to the buyer). The Leader not only sets the benchmark for today, but creates the future legacy of the organization. The Values and Culture exemplified by the Leaders, and all Participants should be handed down from year to year, and to future Leaders.

Owners, hear this loud and clear: YOU are the face and the visual representation of your organization, like it or not. Your management team is your mirror. If your and their personal cultures (Values in Action) do not reflect the Values of the organization, you might as well take a wad of C-4 and attach it to the foundation of your company. Then hand the control wires over to your entire participant population. They will use it, eventually. You cannot hide behind the White House walls or the banners of Morgan Stanley. You are not too big to fail.

As management is the *"Face"* of an organization, and holds dear the Purpose, Values, Integrated (Collaborative) Business Plan and uses Visible Tangible Integrity as its organizational GPS, the essence of spreading those gospels is to **Connect, Engage, Collaborate,** with all potential Participants to the success of the organization. Connect is the touch. Engagement is being fully visible and present, and Collaboration is both asking and answering questions in dialog designed to educate.

The key question in **Connect: Engage: Collaborate** is this: **"What do you think?"** This single, simple question seeks information, insightful opinions, knowledge sharing and acknowledges the value of all people in the conversation. It is especially valuable working with outside vendors and internal resources not typically sought out in that manner. It is an educational moment in that the ensuing conversation will always lead to a discussion of Purpose and Values and Collaborative objectives.

Two of my favorite The Great Workplace chiefs do the following: One wears a blue company work shirt to his highly successful company every day, and seeks out the input of everyone he encounters. He is in corporate videos, newsletters and internal communications. You KNOW that each presentation and newsletter communication is written by him. His videos are mostly unrehearsed, and highly informative. He is involved, on the shop floors, at each division frequently, visible, tangible and straight-forward. He repeats the organization's Values and Purpose at every opportunity. Operations and Executive Management totally reflects his authenticity, without attempting to be his clones. His authenticity resonates now, and will when he decides to pass the baton in the future. It is not so much his personality, but the values, purpose and expectations he reflects.

The second gentleman operates a $700 Million + organization. Before his current company he founded and sold a wildly successful unrelated business. He unabashedly wears *"Harley Davidson"* shirts and jackets to group presentations (with a tie) and speaks directly and truthfully about and on any topic regarding success and his companies. His current company has nothing to do with Harley Davidson; he does. His organization reflects that same openness and directness. No verbal hedging and the organization has achieved enviable annual growth. He is not only visible, but transparent, and genuine; like the motorcycle he rides. His values reflect the organization's values.

Four larger than life examples: Apple and Steve Jobs, Sir Richard Branson and everything *"Virgin"*, Bill Gates and Microsoft, Henry Ford and Ford Motors. Out front, tangible and preaching the values, the why and the future. Like them or not, three of the four are no longer attached to their organizations except in concept, but their organizations stand today.

Will organizations that build on the Icon of their Chief survive and thrive? That's where the solid *"Why"* takes over and the Integrated Business Plan (that includes succession planning) will get its test.

For small- to medium-size organization owners, what are the most evident stumbling blocks in achieving Enduring status?

First, conceptually, separating the WHYS: We all want to make money. We're not socialists. But if you choose making money for yourself above or instead of a true Purpose, organizations will last only as long as your passion for your pocket. Once satisfied, the organization will lag and eventually deteriorate until another worthy, (and greedy?) chief takes over. This is one of the reasons that family organizations disappear upon family succession: the next generation, if not as intrinsically motivated as the founder, and if not able to arrange a new Purpose to the organization, will eventually need to sell assets. I say this with some reservations, as I do know family members who have grown organizations beyond the founder's vision. In each case there was an existing Purpose and an acute sense of How, before the hand-off.

An owner does need to have a selfish reason for the organization's success tied to his or her own self image. We need that to endure the 24/7 of starting up, growing the firm and putting the poles and canvas or skins in order. But smart owners seek to distinguish themselves in a highly Collaborative way: they set a Purpose to attract the Right People to help them grow, they establish the How of their organization in their plans, and they delegate the Hows to an Integrated plan for their entire organization so that they are not one-armed wallpaper hangers. Cosmo G. Spacely (George Jetson's boss at Spacely's Space Sprockets) would not make it as a Leader in the future or today. In golf locker room terms, owners need to stuff their ego in their bag.

Formulating a true Purpose: Many owners are expert at the What of their business. Most have been in business before and have started their own organization based upon technical or personal expertise. They are sure about the What and How. Finding the Why can be a difficult conceptual issue, and many get stuck at How (uniqueness). If the new owner left an organization similar to the one they start, the Why is mostly personal. That is why we have to spend days convincing our spouses WHY it will be okay for the family to endure the new venture. It's not about the vision for the organization, it is personal.

Many new owners or managers have a real issue with knowing where the lofty vision or Purpose should meet the reality of the asphalt. They start with a *"vision"* that is so out of touch with the reasons customers purchase products it might be comical. *"Change the way aircraft manufacturers use Hydraulic Valves for in-flight orientation correction"*. Or, *"Create databases for our customers that will change the way industrial organizations interface with customers around the world"*. They stop at *"Mission-Speak"* rather than "by doing business with us, this is what will change". They stop at defining the How (what is unique about the product or service) and forget that the true Purpose of the organization needs to be lofty, do-able, for ALL participants, especially *"employees"*.

And there is the next block: Employees. Common questions today are, *"What can we say that people will buy into? People today don't care about principles or doing work for someone they cannot see. People are only worried about themselves."* Then why do they go to a place of worship, wear NFL/MLB jerseys, talk about their family, their kids, and their favorite cars? People have a genetic need to identify with an affinity group. You just need a good reason for those people to choose yours. Give them a good reason to wear your company jacket and they will.

You know the What. Design the How. Build the Purpose and Values. Make them public, right next to your ISO Quality posters and above your Mission Statement. Construct the *"Field Manual"* for all operating units and assure Collaboration to seek the Purpose. Hire the Right People, inspire them, and make sure you and management are Visible and Tangible and filled with Integrity. Make every activity one where you Connect, Engage and Collaborate with all Participants.

Enduring is the result of Design, the result of Vision and the result of Hard Work and the Passion that drives the work. But without a firm foundation, those things can be ephemeral.

Not to ignore that *"Sustainability"* (Green) is a key component of Endurance: if your organization is not looking seriously at all facets of Sustainability that you can invoke now, and have planned for the future, you simply have not been keeping up with the press, or you are ignoring your responsibilities to our planet beyond the next year. You probably are still using incandescent lighting.

And while you are focused on all of this, have some fun in the journey. You created an organization, and that was satisfying. Now create your future, the future for your Participants and especially your Customers.

As you seek *"Enduring,"* the fun of it will be in becoming Remarkable. You won't have to say it, everyone else will.

Be Remarkable.

Business Volatility:
The Case for Building The Great Workplace 2.0

Executive Summary:

- Leadership is never just *"easy."* Guiding a small- to medium-sized ship (organization) takes focus and learned skills, and a cool-headed Captain and Crew.
- The ship sails well as long as the Crew BELIEVES in their Captain, and the foundation that has been created that he or she stands upon.
- Remarkable Organizations have solidified a structure, a fluid plan, and simple-to-understand Guiding Purpose and Values to reduce uncertainty in changing environments. Thus the organization Endures.

The true problem with perceived volatility is that it strangles all positive thoughts and actions. The tendency is to sit, worry and wait. We are people after all, not data, our levels of confidence and foresight are our engines and our gyroscope. People need to believe and KNOW that our Values, Actions (Culture), Purpose for doing what we do and our Leadership will win-out, regardless. We also know that the future will not be easy, regardless of the market economy.

A strong Leader must be able to inspire all participants and be inspired by a clear vision regardless of market conditions. Well planned words and speeches are ephemeral. The crew is looking at both the Platform on which the Leader and organization stand and how the Leader interprets that Platform at any time. Today, with Global uncertainty (business, political, leadership) and presidential politics in high gear, words become unintelligible.

The Clear Vision from the Leader defaults to the Enduring Character of the Organization itself. If the organization has been built and has evolved on unshakable Values, Purpose, and Visible Tangible Leadership, the Culture (*Values in Action*) it will be both firm and fluid. It is able to change direction as confident Leadership points the way, reminding everyone (including the Leader) about the Why, the How and the Integrated Business Plan upon which it will function.

If you have not built your organization on the principles and characteristics of The Great Workplace 2.0 you will be guiding your ship without the proverbial rudder.

Creating The Great Workplace 2.0 is as much about the foundation and vision as it is How the Leadership and organization reacts to adversity and the actions it takes on the charge or rebound. They go together. Leadership makes the foundation tangible.

This is an amazing and Remarkable example of reflecting and re-creating a firm foundation: Give-backs, reductions in pay and overtime and knife-cuts to spending/contributions are unfortunately common in manufacturing organizations faced with deep slumps in their customer's economies.

One such Northeast Ohio manufacturer was forced to do all of the above, without invoking life-altering layoffs (good in itself). AFTER the storm settled and business levels returned to black from red, the organization not only returned all give-backs to their normal levels, but PAID BACK every penny that every employee had sacrificed (Including 401K contributions) **WITH INTEREST**. Please re-read that.

That action reflected the deep Values of the organization, their Purpose (beyond making money) and the ultimate example of Visible, Tangible Leadership. That massive and generous response to all involved in the organization cemented an already Enduring foundation for the future.

Don't ask. I will never reveal the organization's identity, or anything that could identify who they are. I keep my word.

This is an example of the opposite: A 75-year old, respected firm stayed in family ownership. The first generation passed it along to the second, with great success. When the second passed it to the third, the deterioration started. Generation #3 was taciturn, lacked the ability to Visibly and Tangibly promote the highly established Values of the organization's history, and let the organization shake as it entered into a more competitive era. The family was wealthy, as was #3. As bad decisions were made, his lack of Leadership began to show and he disappeared from view (Isolation), except when he wanted to complain (Inconsistent Leadership, focus on self). #2 became inconsequential to the organization due to health. Within a few years #3 decided to (when faced with the need to right the ship) sell off divisions, close the main organization, and retreat with his wealth to retirement. He didn't want to lead the company out of turbulent waters. He didn't need to. He also didn't know how. Please know that one of the struggling divisions that were sold off, has now, under Leadership, regained and exceeded their elite status world-wide.

About 1,000 people lost their jobs and hundreds of vendors lost their accounts. The Vision had been lost; right after the Values and Purpose had been forgotten. Even *"C"* level people under the #3 were without rudders and could not/ did not, put the organization in a new path for success.

It did NOT have to be that way. # 2 made a bad, but predictable mistake. #3, wanting his own identity, had allowed the Purpose and Values as the core success of the organization to slip. Lieutenants to # 3 had not been chosen on the principles of the Right People. They were there for jobs and salaries, friends of #3, and not the kind of people to make challenges. No board or outside collaboration took place. No Leadership. No current Values, No Purpose and No plan. In another chapter, we will also refer to this situation when speaking about Intelligent Profitability.

In The Great Workplaces, foundations are made, based upon the 13 characteristics outlined that allow Leadership to Lead, and Engaged (Right) people to follow. When the Right People are Connected and Engaged to the organization and the Vision, Engaged in the Values and Purpose, and are asked to Collaborate (Innovation) for their success and the success of the organization as a whole, the odds of withstanding even the most Volatile market conditions are increased geometrically. It is that foundation that produces Solutions, and Leadership points the way.

One of the descriptors of The Great Workplace 2.0 of TODAY, versus what may have been the norm before organizations of any size were inextricably linked by the *"Global"* economy and its inherent competitiveness, was that the Great Workplace was 'formed in concrete': its structure, products and place in the market were not fluid.

Today, the ability of the organization to be fluid (change, morph, flexible) is critical to survival and growth. Yet, that same organization must have Purpose and Values that are solid, hurricane-proof and beyond reproach. A dichotomy? Perhaps not.

On surface, the dichotomy of Rock Solid and Fluid may seem opposed, but they are not.

The fluidity of an organization to compete today is in its Integrated Operating Plan, founded in Purpose and Values. The plan can change and needs to have built-in re-framing points according to market conditions. It needs to have points of Intelligence (economic predictors, market predictors, knowledge of competition and customers) that are built into the plan and the contingencies that are produced by this knowledge.

Purpose And Values Should Not Change.
To know if your Values and Purpose are solid and can be sent to the engraver to be etched on your trophies for 20 years out, ask this question; *"If we were to completely change product or service lines, would we still hold our Values and Purpose as critical to our success?"* If the answer is no, your Values and Purpose are weak.

Creating or recreating The Great Workplace that will grow, satisfy the customer and weather the worst of storms, even those that are unforeseen, is a product of building a platform ON and BY Purpose. And that is done by working ON your business, not just IN your business. During that building process is where Leadership evolves and takes on its Visibility and Tangibility. When the Platform and the Leadership mirror each other, Endurance is the result.

That platform is the fundamental from which Ray Dalton (PartsSource) would likely say *"Proceed With Confidence"* (The title of his autobiographical book, with a tag line of *"Lessons learned from a serial entrepreneur"*). To extend the need for a foundational Operating Plan further, a *"Rayism"* can be used: *"Never bring someone a problem without offering your idea of how to solve it."*

If you have not read this book, you should. After you are finished, and see its value, go on over to PartsSource and ask Ray to autograph it for you. If he is not on a charitable mission to provide medical equipment to third world countries, he will be flattered.

Your Three-Foot Circle: ™
Are You Playing Bumper Cars With Your Life?

Executive summary:
- *"Your Three Foot Circle"* is an allegory for the sum total of your thoughts, beliefs and pre-actions in your life. It is what makes you, you.
- In regards to business owners, their relationships with Participants to your organization, and the Leadership you exhibit with the intent of having followers, the contents and size of your Three-Foot Circle defines you, within your own thoughts and in the perception of others.

"We don't see things as they are, we see things as we are."
(Anais Nin, French author, or from the Talmud.)

Your Three-Foot Circle. It is where you live. It contains your perspectives on life, the world around you, your opinions, and your *"do's and don'ts. Your "lens on the world"* is attached to it.

Visualize standing in the center of a Hula Hoop. You are standing in your life.

Visualize sitting in a bumper car at an amusement park. Your ride entails purposely bumping into others in identical vehicles. Your action of bumping into another car is the equivalent of making a statement. You see a reaction, but nothing is learned, nothing is gained from either party. Many people do the same with their lives. Not just passing ships in the night, but creating attention or contentiousness.

Inside your three-foot circle is a *"translation"* (Lens) device. It converts all you see and hear to language you understand. It interprets the outside world to terms and concepts that fit within Your World. The device is built upon your logic, rules and opinions.

It is your safe place. It is the cardboard box you climbed into as a child, and it contains your dreams, your fears, and your pleasures.

It is where you hide the idea that YOU should be understood, first and only, and that other people or ideas are simply inconsequential to your life. Or it contains your engine of curiosity, always seeking new information, with few pre-disposed filters between you and new information.

And now it will be the one comfortable place that will stop your development, stop your learning, and stop those who wish to connect with you, from actually connecting and engaging.

Or ... it will be a highly flexible circle, capable of expanding to encompass others, new concepts and ideas that just very well might expand *"who"* you are, the impact you have on others and the impact they can have on you.

With a Three-Foot Circle that is expandable, you will learn, change and grow.

But you will need to reject some of your early training and some of the fears you have, and in many ways the influences you have received that whomever you are today, whatever your thoughts are and whatever your pre-conceived ideas of your Self are, those may be arresting your future growth, happiness and your ability to influence others.

New information is Change, and Change is met with resistance by many of us who think that who we are today is sufficient.

We have all learned this in many ways, but our kids (or you) learned it from Mr. Rogers:

"You always make it a special day for me. You know how, don't you? By just your being you. Whether you're in kindergarten or third grade or no grade at all or ANY grade at all, I like you just the way you are. I'll be back tomorrow. Bye."

Mr. Roger's Neighborhood was a baby-sitting substitute when the kids needed calming or we just needed our own space. The program was mesmerizing to kids. And…we should have watched along with them. Big mistake that we did not.

"Don't Ever Change!" *"We love you just the way you are!"* Live in a fantasyland and everything will be okay. (And, *"don't talk to strangers!!!"*) In other words: Stay in your Three-Foot Circle! Don't venture out, but when you do, it will all be a make-believe world.

Personal growth comes when you flex your three-foot circle to include others', and therefore expand your own reach. It changes and expands your worldview and allows you to understand other points of view, new ideas and new realities. You may discover new ways to live and think, and more often than not, have new *"ah-ha"* moments.

Keeping only within your Three Foot Circle is like playing Bumper Cars with your life. You go around in circles simply bouncing off other people's Three Foot Circles. No Engagement. No Learning. No Growth. No Value.

From Steven Covey's *7 Habits of Highly Successful People*, Habit #5:

"Seek first to understand, then to be understood".

It is the core to expanding your Three-Foot Circle. It is your calling to grow.

And you know those people whose circle is wide: They are the ones who first ask: *"So, what do YOU think?"* or "What has YOUR experience been?"

An organization with many Participants who have expandable, flexible circles, is on its way to being a Great Workplace. They seek knowledge, they seek *"new"*, they seek to understand and learn. They seek to grow. And their Circle (where they live, so to speak) grows with them.

An expanding Three Foot Circle adds new experiences, new opinions, the seeds of Innovation, and the ability to change pro-actions (ideas, opinions and internal rules that cause your actions). It changes your perspective on the world around you It can also confirm your thoughts, opinions and rules.

Being an entrepreneur, owner, or small/ medium size business manager is a tough life, most of the time. It is easy to understand why we feel like a punching bag at the end (or beginning) of many days. And due to that, just to feel safe, many of us retreat into our circles (comfortable, known and warm) just to seek sanity or solace. When we do, we tend to put up a steel circle around ourselves, and shut off the outside world completely, even in a group of *"equals"*.

In my more than 500 meetings with owners and managers of small to medium sized organizations and in my *"networking"* experiences, here are some observations from those who have tiny circles out to those who have transparent and fluid circles around them:

1) **Remarkable:** Those with the most transparent circles have a calm confidence about themselves to the point of not having to prove something in every conversation. This equates to Charisma. The boxing gloves are down, and they seek knowledge and opinions. Their demeanor is relaxed, their eyes are seeking and they are quick to ask: *"What do you think?"* and *"How do you feel about that?"* or even *"What are you looking forward to?"* without prejudgment or deflection. They are *"open"* because they are NOT afraid that others are seeking to find or will find flaws in their character or ideas. But, they still maintain the ability to draw the line on silly conversation. These people seem to love to chat with others with their shoulders squared to the other person, giving the conversation their full attention.

2) **Closed:** People with the smallest, most-protected circles have a habit of responding to your statement or opinion with: *"Yes, BUT ..."* and then stating their opinion with vigor. At the same time they do that, they don't look you in the eyes. They want THEIR opinion or statement to hang in the conversation, on its own. They *"play bumper*

cars" with you. They love to challenge you, and then make more statements. These folks have a tendency to stand at an angle to those with whom they converse. They learn or exchange views and knowledge on little or nothing.

3) **Remarkable:** People with expanding circles ask more questions than others. They seek to understand, they seek knowledge. And you can see their *"mind-wheels"* turning. They ask a question, then question the answer. They dig. And as they learn, their eyes sparkle. They also say *"I didn't know that"* with sincerity. It is a painless form of self-deprecation, and an invitation to go further.

4) **Remarkable:** There are a few people who approach everything with *"the eyes of a child"*; pure wonderment and a huge sponge behind their eyes and ears. They don't try to hide their fascination with *"new"*. They *"Innovate"* right on the spot, with the new information they have received. They love the game of learning. Be prepared to have long conversations with these folks from which you may feel exhausted. You are co-creating something with them.

5) **Closed and guarded:** And then there are those who are in the dead-middle; they respond to questions, guardedly. They will give vague opinions and only ask a few questions. When they leave a conversation, the audience is simply not certain from where they were coming, and will probably never know. They float like a butterfly. No Bee stings. These are the people who go home from a business event and proclaim it a *"waste of time"*. They sought nothing, gained nothing and gave nothing.

Why is this important to an Owner, Leader or Manager?

The best Leaders Connect and Engage (and Collaborate) with others, always looking for new ideas, new experiences from which they can Innovate, and build relationships. If your habits in a business knowledge exchange meeting (any opportunity with other business people, not just the cattle-herd events) are *"closed"* in nature, you will probably be the same way with employees, managers, vendors and the community. You will also set a precedent for your employee-participants in their dealings internally and externally on behalf of your organization. People will *"follow the Leader"*.

In business and in life, the flexibility of your Three-Foot Circle is a choice.

Those who choose to learn from others, those who choose to be proactive in seeking ideas are those people who are or will become Truly Remarkable. And, their organizations will follow.

Author's note: "Your Three-Foot Circle™" is the tile of a book in progress. This work is being written by myself and the members of MasterMind, a small but Remarkable ensemble of entrepreneurs who believe that "Discovery" is essential to success in life and in business.

Employee Focus:
Connect, Engage, Collaborate

Executive summary:

- An organization that has Objectives (Goals, Missions) aligned with Purpose, Values and Value-based Culture will have a firm foundation on which to build Challenges for The Right People.
- Attracting and Retaining Talent can be manageable, when looked at from the perspective of the Talent, not just your demands or desires.
- Remarkable Organizations purposefully build their foundations and ALIGN hiring/ retention systems around the idea of *"Cradle to Grave"* with each new participant.

The very nature of work has changed, including who does it, where, when, how and why they do it. The Right people you seek are also seeking the Right Organization in which to trade their best efforts, for your best efforts.

The concept of work and the *"rules of engagement"* of Participants differ from industry to industry, and from function to function. To make matters a bit more complex, effective Engagement of talent varies according to generation. For the first time in U.S. organized business history, we have three generations working side-by-side, each having different perspectives about work, life and achievement. Wow. Talk about the need for an organization to be Remarkable in its Execution of their Internal Purpose.

Remarkable Organizations have learned to create an organizational brand (the iconic representation of what the organization stands for) that attracts and retains: they start building the organization's foundation using the 13 characteristics of The Great Workplace, while nurturing their human talent, and letting prospective Participants know about it. These organizations include Hiring, Development and Retention of talent into their Unit and Organizational plans and into their Integrated Operating Plans.

A common factor separating Remarkable Organizations from those that are not yet remarkable, is the concept of and systematic attention to *"Cradle to Grave"* talent development. It is based in the organization's Culture. It begins with placing a high Value in talent, acting upon that value consistently, and following through with the promises made to the Talent and subsequently back to the organization itself.

Remarkable Organizations ALIGN hiring and development with their organization's Purpose. They Connect, Engage and Collaborate with Participants.

Organizations that have not achieved that level of commitment typically hire the best available people who will accept the positions available, they do no true Immersion, no assessment of employees' developmental needs, except maybe to address apparent problems, and *"hope"* the relationship lasts long enough to get a few things accomplished.

Organizations that do not meet Remarkable standards give Participants *"Moving Targets"* of Purpose, objectives, development and personal rewards. These organizations have a tendency to make it up as they go.

HOW Remarkable Organizations Accomplish High Engagement, High Performance, and High Retention:

1) Remarkable Organizations first take the proper path in evaluating the Talent profile necessary to accomplish the objectives of the function a person will perform. This is an analytical task, well outlined in our chapter *"The Right People."*

2) Management, Human Resources and unit operations define the challenges afforded to the person in this function. These challenges are aligned with Strategic Goals and Objectives for the Unit, the Organization, and the Purpose of the organization.

3) Understanding that a person should grow their talents and accomplishments in their function, Development opportunities, including training and Mentorship are not only posited, but defined in timelines, resources and expected outcomes. Remarkable Organizations know that the Right People want to develop skills, competencies and outcomes that will satisfy both personal needs and those of the organization. Upward mobility, which includes initiatives, functions and future needs, is planned around individuals and the organizational structure. The deeper the commitment to development, the greater the outcome/payback.

4) Remarkable Organizations not only understand the qualifications, accomplishments and skills of the

prospective Participant (their resume so to speak), they understand the person, as a person (their motivations, desires, fears, will do's and won't do's, as examples).

5) Performance management is committed. Reviews are real, tied to expected outcomes and objectives, and handled in an objective and thorough manner. This also includes follow-up reviews after training and development initiatives. Reviews are both vertical and horizontal (the new term is 360° of Feedback) where the organization's representative(s) reviews the performance of the individual, while the individual also reviews the performance of the manager, Organization and the promises. *"Horizontal"* means that peer evaluations are taken in, put in context and mixed within the performance evaluation. A heavy emphasis is on development, objectives met and readjustment of performance criteria according to reality.

A key component of Performance Management systems is the Aligning of organizational objectives with personal visions of achievement and satisfaction. This assures that work accomplishments and objectives align with personal desires in producing a higher level of satisfaction on both sides. Performance Management/ appraisal Conversations need to include questions that begin with: *"What do you think?" "How does this fit with your personal goals?"* and *"What are you looking forward to?"*

6) The potential *"Cradle to Grave"* career path is defined. Remarkable Organizations have the foresight to see and know what a person can and will need to contribute along a reasonable timeline in their career. *"Cradle to Grave"* means from expected start through to exit time or retirement and all options are built into this plan. Remarkable Organizations can plan for reasonable tenure or complete tenure and adjust unit plans accordingly. Yes, this does mean that Remarkable Organizations know that the Right person may only stay X years and they plan for that eventuality. They also plan for *"forever"* contributors and align their expectations for that as well. There is give-and-take in any projection.

7) Remarkable Organizations have plans and timeframes for developmental training, assignments that will challenge all functions, spin-off assignments designed to grow skills (projects that are tangential to the functional objectives, but will build cross-unit understanding, like internal task forces), and off-site workshops, programs and conferences.

8) All of this is aligned with corporate Purpose and aligned to the Participant's objectives both FOR the organization and the individual's objectives. This pole in the Tipi is straight, continual and Collaborates with all other unit poles.

Remarkable Organizations have plans that Engage talent.

In the chapters *"Right People"* and *"Immersion"* I have detailed that Remarkable Organizations plan Engagement that begins the first time a potential hire is touched, whether via ads, referrals or interviews. The Immersion process begins with Engagement. *"Why"* a person will want to *"take their talent"* to you is fostered in true and complete ways. Remarkable Organizations avoid saying, *"We are a good company to work for."* (Everyone says something like that). And they speak in terms targeted to their audience that align with Purpose, Values and Culture, and that would attract the talent sought to what the organization can and will offer for the present and future. Their Immersion presentations are geared toward having the prospective Participant *"envision"* the experience of joining the staff, accomplishing critical objectives, accepting and accomplishing challenges, being developed and receiving training that results in creating the Future Participant (the person).

"Engagement" is described in many ways, from *"drinking the Kool-Aid"* to understanding HOW the organization's Values and Purpose are to be applied in all things *"work"* as relative to objectives and goals. Engagement is a two-way understanding; both sides' needs are being met. Engagement is designed to Connect, Engage and Collaborate with all people.

Leaders begin the Engagement process with all Participants. It is in their speech, their attitude, their questioning and their responses to questions. Remarkable Leaders understand and practice consistent and frequent references to the organization's Purpose, Values, Missions and Vision. Repetition works. Mick Jagger said it perfectly: *"Anything worth doing ... is worth Overdoing."* If we apply "Brand Marketing" theory to Participant Leadership, marketing says a potential customer needs to hear the brand message 27 times before it sinks in. Leaders need to remember that when they are endeavoring to Engage their participants; mentioning the Purpose, Values and Vision once or twice a quarter will simply not cut it.

Engagement can be seen in the Culture and atmosphere of any organization. It is the *"Feel"* one gets when you walk into the organization. Engaged organizations simply have a heightened level of focused enthusiasm than non-engaged organizations. Purpose, Values, Missions and Visions are no longer terms only in the language of Leaders. It is in the language of the entire Tribe. This common language conveys the meaning of the work to each Participant, and today a very high percentage of the people you want in your organization's Tipi are looking for Real and Tangible Meaning (The Purpose as interpreted by the individual) in the work they do.

Remarkable Organizations understand Generational differences.

Today we can have three maybe even four generations working side by side, not just two. And there are differences between each that need to be understood. These generational differences may be evident on the surface, but when invoking the process of attraction and retention via Engagement, these differences can be critical. These differences in generational Engagement are understood all the way into Performance Management opportunities.

1) The *"New"* generation can appear less engaged in your Purpose and Vision, especially if Purpose and Vision are only posters on a wall. The New generation will "stand back" from concepts of leadership, competition, challenges and recognition, preferring to define those in their own terms. The difference has a thin edge, and does not always apply, but *"Legacy"* (old ways to engage that are considered assumed from older management) engagement may seem to work, when it isn't. Jobs to many of the newest generation workers are viewed as shorter term arrangements, as opposed to the oldest generation, which was brought up thinking that a good job could and should be forever. Though Jobs are viewed by both generations as needing to satisfy individual aspirations, those aspirations vary greatly. *"Millennials"* want their work to have a Purpose bigger than themselves (change the world of ____; contribute to the greater good, etc.), be driven by a *"Dynamic Culture"* (*Values in Action*), and to feel Value (Solid money, invited to participate in the future, rewards of recognition). They want to be included and be asked for their opinion. Remarkable Organizations know

---

[1] These observations are my professional opinions and are not presented here as clinically supported findings, they are my empirical observations.

to personalize the engagement process with the new generation. They get to know these folks very well and speak to them in terms meaningful to each person.

2) *"Less New"* generations (middle) in your workforce can be even more difficult. The *"newness"* of their organization (current employment) has worn off and they have seen the reality versus the promise. Many are ready for increased compensation, skills development and may have become disillusioned with a lack of challenges and growth. In other words they have tried, been held back or not recognized and feel of lower value. Those realities need to be addressed directly, openly and honestly with these folks to accomplish engagement, and it will take time and proof of what you are offering to accomplish that.

3) The *"Older"* generation folks tend to become more engaged with Purpose and Values, and can easily visualize their contributions to your Purpose. In many ways it is still about them as individuals, and recognition needs to be true and consistent. Growth is a good thing, but stability, respect and the feeling of being Valued are at the top in motivations. They can see that the New Generation is fawned upon, and perhaps feel less appreciated. Remember that this *"Older"* generation was influenced early on by work ethic, competition and doing the *"right thing."* Immersion and development needs to target their openness and willingness to get the job done. But lie to them about anything, and they will walk out … mentally and possibly physically, too.

These differences are meant to be points of guidance, and not resolute to any individual. Remarkable Organizations are able to personalize their Immersion, Development and Performance

Management processes to these assumptions. Doing so increases productivity, career satisfaction, retention and payback.

All generations are seeking non-moving targets (objectives) in the work they do and the rewards they can look forward to.

Remarkable Organizations have market-based compensation plans.

Turnover is costly, and it is a given in most organizations. HR preaches it, CEOs know it, some management attempts to avoid turnover, which becomes even more costly.

Paying lower than the market may look like an effort to decrease costs. No one wants to spend more than they have to spend, especially in recurring costs, like salaries and hourly wages.

Remarkable Organizations analyze compensation, and fit their offerings to their ability to *"invest"* in talent, the market and the current trends. Salary surveys are good starting points, but even the best surveys are trailing averages, arranged by *"Titles"* (which may vary dramatically from your specific functions), geography, tenure, industry, and other *"bucket-style"* classifications (it doesn't fit anywhere else, throw it in there).

There are countless Human Resource-based organizations and institutes who offer statistics on compensation. Government-based information tends to be, well, government style: all-encompassing, general and confusing. Salaries tend to be all over the map (ex: Administrative Assistant, Level 4: Salary; $15,000 to $45,000 depending upon the industry....blah, blah, blah).

Local to Northeast Ohio, we have an organization that offers industry and even YOUR industry-based research, both general and targeted for YOU. This is the venerable Employer's Resource Council (ERC). ERC offers a continual, knowledge-rich look at building and developing Great Places to Work. They consult on compensation, benefits, HR best practices and much more. They are the founder of the prestigious NorthCoast 99 Award (Best places to work in NE Ohio).

Full disclosure is needed here. The CEO of ERC is Pat Perry, whom I admire and respect greatly, we met when we were both at AIM Executive Search (THE best damn search firm ever, which was eventually sold to Interim Personnel/ Spherion for a huge bag of money). I left AIM to buy Champion about the same time Pat left to head ERC. Champion studied the NorthCoast 99 qualifications and has been a multiple-time award winner. Thank you to Pat Perry for guiding Champion on our way to excellence. During that same time Champion achieved multiple Weatherhead 100 Awards (Fastest growing privately held companies in NE Ohio) along with countless awards for service excellence, growth and quality. ERC has been a component of our excellence and can offer the same to almost any organization. ERC, the NorthCoast 99 award and Pat were also motivators for me to pursue a slightly different look at Remarkable Organizations and create the continuing study that has resulted in this book, and the sequels to come.

ERC offers a comprehensive full-cycle Human Resource development consulting service that small- to medium-size organizations should look into. One of those components is salary data and analytics. They will put your compensation and benefit plans where they need to be, and help develop your organization to become Remarkable.

Remarkable Organizations pay well. Some pay the best. None pay below the market, unless there are other bonuses, benefits and unique factors to attract and retain darn good people. There will always be an organization willing to pay one individual more to come aboard than any other organization, but typically that is a one-time deal where blanket pay in that organization is not at the exceptional level. And that usually comes in a *"signing"* or *"contract"* bonus. One-time cost or investment, as it may be.

Remarkable Organizations have achieved or are achieving a balanced pay/benefits/bonus plan that attracts and retains the quality people their organization's Integrated Operating plan dictates. Their pay reflects the value of each employee and the function they hold. Their benefits reflect the value of entering into a *"contract"* not only with the individual, but the family.

Remarkable Organizations do not capitalize on a prospective employee's unemployment and offer less than market. They know that *"Attitude"* starts with the details.

Remarkable Organizations keep and Develop good Managers and extricate *"Bad Mangers"*:

The #1 reason people leave organizations is Bad Management. Most of people's claims are very true, albeit some are made-up excuses for their own poor performance, and people do leave positions claiming "Bad Management" before being fired by Good Managers. Other top reasons people exit organizations include: limited promotional opportunities, pay, job boredom and lack of challenge.

My Perspective on this has a foundation in the Staffing and Search profession. Over my time in this profession, our companies have placed people in over 7,000 Northeast Ohio organizations, 60,000 people through retained search, direct-hire positions and many hundreds of thousands in interim and interim-to-direct hire assignments. We consult with organizations needing to contract or hire industrial, warehouse, office, technical, management, staff and executive-level people. We have staffed organizations from the ground floor up (yes, from *"Zero"* employees to over 150 employees including all staff, management and hourly, hired by me) to hiring and managing staffs over 200 employees, on site).

I have been personally involved with the good, bad and severely ugly reality of hiring and retention. Having our organization's quality based upon ISO 9001:2000, being in business 24/7, allows us to hear intimately, the dual feedback from employees and managers. We deal with owners, managers and Human Resources on a daily basis. Our/ my experience and actionable knowledge would equate to the sum total of the *"Q"* arena filled with HR professionals, or to bring in a Native perspective, the number of Warriors Custer didn't expect at Little Bighorn.

Different than the management/ HR perspectives in most organizations, we hear BOTH sides of the turnover story, and try to sort out the reality. Combine that with my meetings with Leaders of organizations for this book, we/ I do have a substantial foundation.

Here is the main conundrum organizations are faced with when they discover less than good employee management and supervision: *"How can we fire a technically superior person, who has lower than needed management skills, when we have no internal backup?"* *"We just have to live with Fred's unique style, because he knows more about his department than anyone in the organization, including the owner?"* *"We need to be careful with Susan, she knows HOW to make Accounting hum."*

Do you fire and take a step back in technical competencies, or live with turnover, lower than perfect productivity and the constant employee relations issues, including potential litigations?

Remarkable Organizations don't live with poor managers. They begin by choosing these people carefully either in the recruiting or promotion process. An Organizational Values, Purpose and Culture match MUST be present. There is no room for guessing or being close. References are checked thoroughly, and pointed questions about *"style"*, attitude towards people and their development are the topics of the day.

Remarkable Organizations will use practical examples of supervisory circumstances and ask, *"How HAVE you handled these issues in the past?" "Would you change your approach?"* And more. And then they re-check references to pinpoint reality versus *"Interview answers"*.

When promoting people to their first management position, great care is taken to separate technical competency from management skills. The tendency for most organizations is to promote the most knowledgeable person first or to hire a person based upon their technical skills, without looking at their management suitability. Management can be a more difficult skill to evaluate than hard skills like Accounting, Engineering, or Process knowledge.

In any management hire and especially in management promotions Remarkable Organizations do these things right:

1) Prescreen for Values, Purpose and Culture match. Does the person identify personally and professionally with your expectations? Check references.

2) Know the person, as a person, not just lines on the resume. Recruiters call this *"reading the white spaces"* on the resume. People have a tendency to do things for their reasons (personal points of view, refer to our chapter on Your Three-Foot Circle), not yours.

3) Use assistance from learned, psychological evaluation organizations. One such organization in Northeast Ohio is PRADCO (Chagrin Falls). They have the ability to customize their evaluations to your environment and expectations.

4) Define *"proper management"* within YOUR organization, and make a ballpark template about it.

5) Remarkable Organizations understand, look for and develop supervisors and managers with high Emotional Intelligence (EI) and an innate or learned ability in Appreciative Inquiry (AI). EI is defined as: the ability to identify, assess, and control the emotions of oneself, of others, and of groups. For Dr. Cooperrider's overview of AI through Appreciative Inquiry Commons at Case Western Reserve University, check http://appreciativeinquiry.case.edu

Benefits. ObamaCare is really muddying the waters on this one, but in most cases is only affecting the *"bottom"* of the requirements as our country moves ever so slightly toward *"Socialism."* All personal opinions aside, Remarkable Organizations DO execute their benefits and employee welfare programs differently than others.

In the chapter *"Intelligently Profitable,"* the case is made for organizational Investment in its own future. People are your present and future. Your people have their own stability and security as prime motivators and are looking to their employers to be sensitive to their needs and wants.

It is really this simple: if your employees are worried about protecting themselves, family and extended family, they can't and won't be able to focus 100% on their work or Purpose. People always think about *"what if"* when it comes to health and the coverage of unknowns becoming real in their lives.

Remarkable Organizations invest in their people's lives and needs. It is not out of a need to be generous; it is out of a connection to Purpose and future. It is a competitive advantage in the search for and retention of talent.

The organizations I have touched that are in fact in the Remarkable category do not lack in any benefit category. Some are very innovative (for Northeast Ohio and our old line manufacturing base) and some are copying the leaders of their own industries (Silicon Valley). All take good care of their Participants.

I won't presume to advise on benefit plans other than to say the following: research your industry standards, your local benchmarks to be competitive, and have a third-party benefits consulting firm advise you. Be competitive, be realistic.

One example of an organization who could make the list of Remarkable (eventually) but has a major hurdle to overcome, in benefits: In a specialty field they are a true player. The owner/ founder has been Entrepreneur Of The Year in his industry's category. They are profitable and they are growing. A solid core of individuals has been employed there long-term, in some part due to the lack of competitive organizations in the area. But when a new person is hired on, they are told from the outset NOT to take the company-offered benefit plan. The current employees will tell that person where to buy their own, with the alternative cash offered by the company if a person does not take the company's plan. The difference between appropriate company-offered benefits versus the cash offered could not reduce profit to a loss (that assumption is based upon known sales volume). So close, yet so far.

Work-Life Balance is critical. And this can be a product of the industry the organization is in. High-stress environments in

Remarkable Organizations find relief points for employees and management alike. Relief Points doesn't necessarily mean avoidance of stress as much as it points to the ability to achieve desired objectives, and be recognized for that. Relief Points are also rewards that signify achievements of meaningful objectives.

Balance is about doing meaningful things in and outside of work that achieve personal satisfaction and a sense of general well being for the individual. Each side of the equation influences the other.

Take this example: You have a list of things to accomplish, work-related or personal. You make up the ubiquitous *"check list"* of those items, perhaps using a pre-printed empty square followed by a line where you write the task to be achieved. After accomplishing that task you get to put a large *"checkmark"* in the empty box, perhaps stroking that checkmark with great flair. How do you feel? You feel good. Why? Endorphins. Satisfactory accomplishment of tasks can release these *"chemicals"* into your system and produce a minor feeling of euphoria, an instant reward. You feel good, relaxed and accomplished. Life is good.

In The Great Workplace, the organization has aligned goals, objectives, purpose and review of accomplishments with rewards, either tangible or conceptual. There is a payoff for the efforts. These do not have to be trophies or money, but a recognition that is the equivalent of a checkmark. It can be subtle or impactful. If using cash as a reward, the amount is less important than the reward itself.

Remarkable Organizations understand that *"Life Happens"* and make room for flexible allowances:

Family events, personal downtime and involvement in charitable interests not only happen, but should be encouraged and supported. Remember that hiring and retention is *"trading one's best efforts for another's."*

Health and Wellness programs are no longer debatable. Healthy, happy and fulfilled participants simply perform better at work, at home and are less costly (insurance premiums) than those who are not. Great Workplaces insure and protect individuals and families from the effects of health issues. Now the movement is to Assure that those same folks are minimizing current and future health issues.

ALL insurance carriers offer education in and guidance on preventative health programs, including smoking cessation, drug and alcohol abuse and physical fitness. These insurance carriers also offer direct-to-enrollee advice and education on known health issues of the participant. It is simply prudent to support the carrier's efforts by company-wide communications of the same.

Physical and emotional support programs are a staple in Remarkable Organizations from in-house fitness centers to fitness memberships or discounts to encouragement of group participation in Cancer walks, team sports and mental health consultations. These do not have to be expensive nor intrusive to the workday. Your Human Resource professional will have, if that person is a participating member in SHRM (Society for Human Resource Management), excellent actionable knowledge in this area.

Celebrations and acknowledgments should not be confined to individual Performance Reviews. After all, your organization is a Tribe isn't it?

Remarkable Organizations look for every opportunity to acknowledge results, contributions, milestones and victories not only of the organization, but of the individuals in the Tribe.

Participants are brought together to boost familiarity, group and individual prideful accomplishments and simple socialization (which can serendipitously lead to collaboration and Innovation).

Group gatherings, unit gatherings and group socializations confirm Affinity (we are all in this together) and develop in-reach and outreach opportunities leading to better understandings of each other (numbers on phone extension lists now become faces with personalities and passion, as well as the acknowledgment that the extension # is actually a real person). Smart organizations invite key vendors and board members to these events. C-level and upper-level management are encouraged to reach out to as many attendees as possible and not cluster in their own, safe clans.

The extent of these gatherings depends upon the ability to invest (Intelligently Profitable). But a word of caution: Holiday parties (the old model of *"open bar"*) are invitations to disaster.

A useful form of group gathering and communications without travel or high expense is in scheduled organization newsletters. These can be in print or published via private access on the organization's website.

The most remarkable newsletters I have seen are deep in content and have tons of photos of individuals who have contributed to the organization in some way. Everyone loves to see their picture and name in print! It affirms the Affinity. In those same remarkable newsletters the CEO makes personal acknowledgment of company and individual accomplishments, industry happenings, future missions and competitive comparisons.

Internet-based gatherings and newsletters capitalize on video content of CEO messages to the Tribe, new product or process introductions, new-hire introductions, group or unit messages to the entire organization. In one such case, unit groups dispersed about the country hold an annual video contest to show the members of each group in an amusing and thematic way. It shows Organizational camaraderie, real people having fun and supporting the entire organization's quest for excellence.

Here is a unique way to gather people who are far apart for Celebrations: The headquarters of a smaller, but global organization gathers their 40 or so corporate participants in a *"ballroom"*. Surrounding the gathering space are TV-sized monitors with Internet video cameras that connect the outliers to the main group and allow interaction between them. Both sides Connect and Engage with each other. Affinity without physical presence. It's a new day!

The newsletters, video and content always repeat Purpose, Values, Culture and Missions. Repetition invokes solidarity.

Remarkable Organizations Connect, Engage and Collaborate with all Tribal members on a regular basis. It solidifies the Organization and Individual pursuits of Purpose. It is the glow and the warmth from the fire in the center of your Tipi where people gather.

Innovation:
It's on and by Purpose

Executive summary:

- Innovation in Remarkable organizations is born from a Passion for Purpose. Passion is both thoughtful and emotional.
- *"Why"* you do what you do for the Customer (and prospective customers) and the Customer's Customer, proceeds to *"How"* (your differentiators) and your How is fueled by the question: "In what ways can we improve (our offerings, for the customer)?"
- Innovation is also directly in front of you, quelled only by your or your organization's view of the world of Possibilities. Innovation is no longer just *"I think"*, but the Collaborative notion of *"We think."*

Innovation does not necessarily have to *"change the world"* to be meaningful or to matter. It is not confined to product or service; it can be in processes, systems, bottlenecks or recurring issues. We tend to think about Innovation in terms of a new mobile phone, tablet PC or some totally new "Amazing" product or service that we look at and say to ourselves, "Why didn't think of that?".

Sometimes little tweaks to an already good product or tinkering a customer service process can be of great significance to the customer, be that *"customer"* external or internal to your organization.

Innovation is not necessarily the domain of one person who came up with the original product, process or idea. It is rare to have that original person be capable of Ideation, Clarification, Development and Implementation of the raw Vision. Some Innovators do in fact see the original idea straight through to the point of sale. Their Innovation may be great, but it may also be cost prohibitive, impossible to make or even already made by a competitor.

Innovations that are implemented, have been through various filters (cost, practicality, resources available, market timing) before they become tangible, and that is where Collaborative Innovation holds dominion: Different perspectives all working on the same opportunity. Collaboration is not Teamwork, even though various *"Teams"* can work collaboratively.

In Remarkable organizations Purpose, Values and appropriate Missions form the foundation to allows Innovation to flourish. Without a targeted Purpose, innovations become *"Inventions"* seeking a customer. Purpose is for the customer, and it comes from the customer. It is not Innovative, unless a Customer agrees it is.

Remarkable organizations have clarity in their Purpose, Values and Missions (the *"Why"* and the *"How"*) The *"What"*, as product or service, can now change with new ideas, even though the Purpose and Values do not.

With this Clarity, Remarkable organizations become intimately close with their customers, almost customers, prospective customers and the offerings of the *"competition."* They seek to understand every nuance of customer feedback.

Here is where your *"Culture"* (Values in Action) pays you back: Any person who touches the Customer, almost customer, prospective customer or the person who researches the competition, must be Passionate about the organization's Purpose (the customer) and trained to listen, observe and analyze the feedback. It is there that Innovations take form in the ways of suggestions, disappointments, and, *"Gee I wish it could do…."* And, *"we are considering ABC's product or service, along with yours."*

When you discover that your offering may not be as Remarkable as you thought, Creativity and Innovation should begin. Remarkable organizations are rarely *"too late"* for Innovations due to having been close to their Customers, Industry Intelligence and competitor's offerings.

Innovative Culture comes from having established Connectivity and Engagement around Purpose, Values and Missions enlisting the entire organization into being *"Scouts"* in your marketplace. Feedback is encouraged to be continual and all findings are given their due audience.

Now, the Vendors: The typical organization *"buys"* things from a source selected upon quality, delivery and price, and they do this in a quick, arm's-length fashion (I like to think of the Heisman Trophy, runner with ball tightly cradled and stiff arm out to ward off tacklers).

Most buyers fear if they get too close or friendly with a Vendor, it may cost them in price or in flexing the rules needed to be set for the Vendor. This gets very evident when there are sealed bids put out, or worse, Internet-based auctions where no human-to-human conversations take place. My own organization was asked to bid in a reverse eBay-style auction for recruiting Physicians! Doctors!?! The auction started at a pre-set price level and then Vendors bid DOWN the price. If there were two vendors left at the close, the auction would then go into a *"5-Minute Overtime"*, and so on. We didn't bid, preferring to remain as professional about our Value as we could. I am not sure I would like to be admitted to a hospital where *"Cheap"* and *"Doctor"* were used in the same sentence.

Remarkable organizations do two things with Vendors: 1) Encourage the best Value based upon needed factors of the buy, and 2) Ask the Vendor "What do you think?" and "What do you know that could help us achieve our Purpose or Mission for OUR Customers?" They involve the vendor in the success of the organization. They Collaborate. They treat the Vendor as a Participant to the success of the organization and their Customers, not a bid sheet.

Just as a Remarkable organization Connects and Engages with their employees for success, they realize the wealth of knowledge a Vendor may have, and fold that Vendor into their Tribe, albeit with a temporary Enrollment card. They encourage the Vendor to Innovate their offerings to the organization and therefore the organization's Customer. They Collaborate. Vendors are invited into the Tipi to sit by the Fire, and share stories of their journeys.

Not all Innovation today has to be fostered internally. P&G now has over 60 percent of their new products developed by external Collaboration.

"Open Innovation" (external Innovation) can be seen locally at Nine Sigma, (www.ninesigma.com) where organizations seeking solutions, Innovations or help on *"How To"*, take their needs to Nine Sigma who in turn enlists the aid of pre-qualified Solution Providers on a confidential basis. This can be done on a targeted basis (brought only to those organizations that fit exact criteria) or on a more Open basis (brought to a broader

spectrum of potential solution providers). Nine Sigma, a group of highly professional solution thinkers themselves, guides the client from start to finish on each project.

On a more turnkey level there is Nottingham Spirk, a virtual Grand Slam hitter in the world of Innovations that can turn an entire industry. John Nottingham and John Spirk have been together since their days at Cleveland Institute of Art, and have built their firm on more than *"1,000 patents and billions of dollars in sales for large, publically owned firms and entrepreneurial start-ups alike."* (over 1,400 clients). They offer full-cycle Innovation, product or prototype testing and launch, and market research. (www.nottinghamspirk.com)

Colleges and Universities can offer Solutions and Innovations where organizations may not have internal expertise. Be very specific in choosing institutions to help based upon their expertise and public willingness. Most universities will tell you their limits and capabilities right up front and the *"cost of entry"* to their hallowed halls.

Affinity Groups of business people can lend expertise on most any topic. The Entrepreneurs Association at John Carroll University offers a unique and confidential program to its 250 business-owner-members: The Business Advisory Network (BAN). If a member needs help with any part of their business operations or in their personal/ professional life, the issue or opportunity is brought to the chair, and then *"expert members"* are invited to join the solution discussions. This not an informal chat over coffee, held between business meetings. It is taken very seriously and is a Collaborative effort for all involved. The results have been Remarkable. Solutions have been provided, affirmations for the path of the person bringing the question(s) to the table and Innovations have happened. Members represent all industries and professions from a minimum of $1 million in sales to over $750 million in sales.

Customers can be an exceptional source of Collaborative development. Your fear might be in showing that you need help from a close Collaboration, you might be showing weakness. In an open and honest discovery conversation, you will both be able to tell the advantages to both parties, without fear of showing your possible weaknesses. This works well when the product or service is first tailored to the Customer, but agreements are made that subsequent offerings (to competitors) do not have the same specifically tailored elements, or do not pose a competitive threat to your first Customer.

Many Remarkable organizations organize their own Collaborative projects with chosen insiders and outsiders. Outsiders can be respected contacts, community business icons, hired consultants, legal firms, accounting firms, vendors and board members. Insiders are chosen with care according to their willingness to contribute, passion for Purpose and their expertise within the organization. Then those are culled for creativity, thoughtfulness and propensity to be identified as: Ideator (full of creative input, *"what if?"* These people may *"irk"* you in normal life, as they can be challenging and annoying), Clarifier (puts ideas and targets into useful perspectives, cautiously), Developers (Refiners) and Implementers (move things forward). Now, there is only the Facilitator to choose.

Facilitators are not content experts. Those experts can sway the conversations toward their own comfort zone. Facilitators are experts in getting agreements on the Purpose of the collaboration (is it end-result oriented, discovery oriented or at a stage of sharing knowledge? Set the stage), encouraging people to share ideas without reprisal, follow through with idea stages and next steps, and to solve process issues. They are great communicators and thoughtful, and have the professionalism to show no obvious bias for the end result. Quite a tall order? In every organization there will be several from which to choose.

Collaborations produce Innovations through sharing of knowledge, sharing of creative ideas and the inclusion of multiple *"points of view."* Collaborations are also, by their very nature, an opportunity for people to be challenged, inspired, and to dream a little. It is a time where people are asked their opinion on something other than their direct job functions and by this inclusion, they will feel more Connected to an entire organization.

Innovation in Remarkable organizations comes from Passion for Purpose, seeing the future today and a focus on creating that future. It comes from allowing and encouraging input from a myriad of sources. It comes from listening and asking probing questions. It can also come from people and places you would not normally consider. It can come from the obvious and from *"beyond the obvious."*

The MAJOR stumbling block to Innovation is when Participants, leaders and followers view *"possibilities"* (ideas or experiences out of the norm) from their own three-foot circle. This is the standard view of the world each of us takes. We filter new information based upon our known information. If the new experience or information does not align with our own base, our opinions, our prejudices and our expectations, we tend to ignore it or reject it.

When we believe the earth is flat, and someone proves that it isn't, we fight it and stare in disbelief. Then we take a few hundred years to change our minds. Dad didn't like Ford automobiles, so neither did I, until I drove a rental. Then I bought number one, two, and then number three.

The same holds true with Innovations, new ideas and paths to Innovations.

Be the person who looks for *"New," "Different"* and *"Better"* with the *"eyes of a child,"* full of wonderment, discovery and Passion. Remarkable organizations have that as part of their Culture (*Values in Action*) and their Purpose.

Observations and Admonitions

As stated earlier in this work; there are NO perfect organizations when compared to the list of 13 characteristics present in The Great Workplace 2.0. Each organization and its leadership does its best to create the best company they can.

As the writer and compiler of sensitive information from mostly privately owned organizations, I feel compelled to share both professional and personal thoughts about my discoveries. I hope that these Observations and Admonitions will add insight into the vast pool of information contained within this work. If these musings seem to repeat the content from some of the chapters, there is a solid reason for it.

Observations and Admonitions:

1) Effective Leadership is consistent, calm and passionate. Many are called and few are chosen to lead. People (followers) can spot disingenuous leaders a kilometer away. Don't attempt to be Steve Jobs or General Patton if you are not, but BE someone who does NOT keep people at arm's

length. The single most prevalent characteristic of *"average at best"* leaders is the Three-Foot Circle they keep around themselves. It is impenetrable. They walk around with *"stay away"* tattooed on their foreheads and the atmosphere they carry with them screams: *"I am not going to open up to you, no matter who you are."* Being guarded 24/7 is defeating the idea of learning and growing. Average leaders, although they may be experiencing some measurable success, never ask the question: *"So, what do YOU think?"* Guys and Ladies: It isn't a hide-and-seek game, and not everyone wants to find your weak spot. Relax, and be real. It won't hurt.

2) The #1 reason people leave organizations is not *"Career Development"* as they tell you when resigning or in an exit interview. It is Bad Management. I have personally visited more than 400 manufacturing and non-manufacturing organizations in the last 6-7 years as a writer or as a consultant. Clearly 50 percent of the first-, second- and third-level line managers (and HR *"Specialists"*) I have met need to be fired or sent to management training schools. It is appalling what some *"Owners"* must think of their workers, that they actually hire or promote goons into supervisory positions, and then expect top performance from the *"Help"* (*"Row faster, you dogs! The Captain wants to water ski!"*).

3) Don't ever call an Interim Worker a *"Temp"* and hold them at arm's length like a leper. When you do, you will have caused that worker to give you, at best, a 50 percent effort. Respect and good leadership can increase a worker's output by multiples. Interim workers typically have the worst jobs in a facility, and they know it. Help them WANT to do a good job, even for the little money they take home. Help them feel a little better about what they do, so they feel better about YOU and themselves.

4) Remarkable Organizations create a Culture. You can feel it, like a heart beat. You sense it the moment you walk in. Culture is Values in Action, and their Values are real. Many almost-Great Workplaces are close but only talk about Values and Purpose when pressed to do so. Talk about them frequently. Owners and Managers who don't talk about Values and Purpose are most likely NOT LIVING the Values on the wall. And guess what; your people know it. If you are not preaching and living your organization's values, leave the Mercedes at home.

5) Innovation comes from Passion. Innovative ideas come from people who feel free to express those ideas and feel certain that those ideas will be heard and evaluated with some level of serious inquiry. True Collaboration is the engine for free thinking, as is a culture of Purpose. Not knowing how to facilitate Culture and Collaboration is not an excuse. Just *"Google"* those terms. There are HUNDREDS of books and whitepapers available to guide you.

6) Managers and Leaders: David Cooperrider (Case Western University) is a world-recognized Guru on the topic of Appreciative Inquiry; look for the best in people. A few hours with his works will positively change your entire approach to working with people. Begin here: http://appreciativeinquiry.case.edu/.

If you have *"Bad Managers"* who are causing bottlenecks, buy them an iPad and YOU download the books to it. $650 is less than the cost of the turnover they created, just last week. Have them give you formal book reports and a plan of how they will use what they learned. Then let them keep the iPad. If they don't complete the assignment, take it back, give it to their assistant. Message received.

7) Your organization isn't Walmart. Treat Vendors with respect; learn from them by asking their opinions and insight. Treat Vendors like you want to be treated. It isn't a contest, it is a relationship. Don't lie to them and don't hide important information from them so that you seem harder to sell.

8) Clean up your entire workplace! The Top Great Workplaces are clean and orderly. There is a direct correlation of Great and Clean.

9) Display your Values and Purpose(s). Your awards from the Boy Scouts are nice, but that only means your Son was one. Your ISO Certificate is meaningless if Customers don't come to see you.

10) Tomorrow won't get better if you keep doing the same things that got you to where you are, and you don't like where you are. Hopes and wishes are not strategic plans.

11) Your Human Resource person needs to spend time doing factory or office jobs. Being a Waiter/Waitress or volunteer in college does not count; they need to know the jobs that the people they service are doing, and not from a spreadsheet. One of the best HR managers I know operates a forging machine, and trains people in QC. She knows what it takes to be good at any job in the factory. She looks good in grease.

12) Your Human Resource person(s) needs to be trained in hiring. Send them to a Recruiting firm to be trained on this critical component. Pay the firm for the training, it's a bargain. Neither colleges nor SHRM seminars train this. Have them read Hire With Your Head by Lou Adler. The $20 you spend on this book will save you tens of thousands of dollars by learning the difference between the Right People to hire and the Wrong People to avoid.

13) Stand back from your organization and think about it, review it and analyze it. Is it a Great Workplace? Why, why not? What could it be? If you can't do this at work or at home, get a nice hotel room for a day. Don't bring your laptop. Bring a legal pad, and start to re-imagine the organization as though it was your original start up. Bring water, no booze, take a nap and keep the TV off. Stare at the walls and the ceiling. Take a shower, take a walk. Immerse yourself in your creative thoughts. Don't order room service. It's too expensive.

14) Join a group of entrepreneurs (in Cleveland, try the JCUEA). Find a Mentor. Buy someone a cup of coffee and talk about how other people have created Great Workplaces. You are not an island. Admitting you are lost or confused is not a flaw and it will cause the other guy to do the same. And, you will help each other.

15) Always remember that *"BIG"* is not remarkable. It's simply BIG. Don't get the idea that what Apple does can be duplicated by you. The same for G.E. or Exxon. They spend more money on coffee in one day than you bill in one year.

16) Read. *A Lot*. But don't try to follow the lectures in books where the author has met with Fortune 100 CEOs. They live in a different world. What they say about Great Workplaces and the organizations they have built becomes public record, and it better be impressive or they will get canned by their Board. Use the information as guidance and inspiration. But you probably cannot duplicate what they do with their 60,000 employees in your 20-person company. They have minions, you have real people. They hire Harvard B-School guys and gals. You have folks who graduated

from Bowling Green and Bedford High School. The BIG guys are driving Battleships in the rough waters; while you are trying to keep a bouncing Zodiac on course. Nevertheless, feel darn good that when you turn the wheel, the boat turns, NOW. The BIG guys have to wait a full fiscal cycle to go to starboard or port.

17) *"Stay thirsty, my friend."* Did you know that beer commercial was actually telling you to moderate? Steve Jobs and The Whole Earth Catalog said: *"Stay hungry, stay foolish."* Thirst for more, but don't read your own press clippings too often. Keep your eyes open and *"observe everything as you walk your path in life."* An Elder taught me that sacred admonition in the Lakota language: *"Akita Mani Yo."* It means more in the Indian language. Call me and I'll explain it to you.

18) Have some fun, manage your personal habits and try to stay healthy. Your followers need you. Thank your deity for the challenges he trusts you to handle on his/her behalf. Thank your family. Laugh often, smile a lot and give some of your time to helping others succeed. Find a good theme song to your life, put it on your Smartphone and listen to it once in awhile. It will remind you why you are doing all this, 18-hours per day, seven-days a week. Sleep is overrated.

19) Read the last chapter in this book. Those two words are the real secret to success.

Future Work:
The Great Workplace 3.0

Executive Summary:

- The next iteration of The Great Workplace has already begun, quietly. You have built your Great Workplace around Purpose and Values and have developed a *"Tribal"* Culture that is productive and aligned. You are focused on your Customer, and your Customer's Customers. Your foundation is solid. It works, on Purpose, by Purpose.

- The world around you is changing quickly, and you will need to Adapt to and Anticipate those changes, at the speed of thought. You have the foundation to do so.

What is coming?

The search for *"Medicine Men and Medicine Women"*: Keep reading please and the analogy will become practical, and its applications evident. In Native or Indigenous communities there are special people called Medicine People (Lakota=Pejuta Pahta). They solve problems, suggest *"medicines"* and advise on potential future outcomes. These unique folks will never offer that they are people who *"Walk with Medicine Bundle"* and when asked, typically defer in their answer by saying simply, *"I may have some special knowledge that is useful."* Medicine people seem to have a grasp on the seen (evident) and on those elements that are beyond the obvious. They are able to **make sense of** empirical data (provable) and the abstract or transcendent. They find **meaning** in it all and are able to apply that meaning as **Healing** (adjustments, solutions).

The corresponding people in business environments have high cognitive skills and are imbued with trans-disciplinary talents. They are able to make sense of disparate and varied input. When they read a page of words, they pull understanding not just from the black print but also out of the white spaces around the words. They use their cognitive and analytical skills with heightened intuition. To many observers, they have *"Vision"*.

These business **Medicine People** are the new *"Right People"* for the future. Their talents will be deployed in analytic functions, R&D, customer service, management, strategic functions, and Human Resources, even if their main functional duties are in production areas (get the work out, processes, and other maintenance/ keep a function up-to-date and flowing).

A critical function where advanced or Social Intelligent and trans-functional skills will be applied is in Human Resources. Although necessary to the effective functioning of The Great Workplace, the HR function has been sorely underutilized. The majority of new HR *"Professionals"* are well-educated and capable of high cognitive utility. What they are missing is Operations experience, where a view of the business environment from the inside out can be garnered. This is in part due to their own legacy needs to focus on administration and specialized functions. Operations experience should be required within The Great Workplace such that any new HR person spends time in the functions they will support, being hands-on, elbow-deep in grease if need be. The majority of HR practitioners can handle the compliance functions associated with their duties, but will only gain the status of Remarkable when their trans-functional skills, social intelligence and Collaborative skills are put into the game.

Modern Medicine people are not self-confined to a personal and protected *"Three-Foot Circle."* They will be the *"seekers"* of New, and the seekers of Vision; they will look for new answers to old questions. They will have various skills and talents, not just a single, well-developed knowledge base.

Favorite thoughts and questions these people ask are: *"In what ways can I/ we help X?"* Or, *"In what different ways can we approach this issue, and exceed expectations for Y?"* *"What if I/ we change X?"* *"What are you/ we looking forward to?"* *"If we dissected this to root components or issues, what would it look like?"* *"If we started from scratch, what would a better alternative look like?"* These people think and live in what if... constructs.

Their approach to the future will be Engaging and Collaborative. They view Collaborative learning as critical to their personal development and rightfully equate that to their own value in an organization. A key factor of connecting successfully with the New Business Medicine People will be to Involve them with both micro- and macro-views of your business and keep them involved. This is not only their path to Challenges, it is their path to self actualization.

New Management talent will be developed from this pool of people as organizations begin to realize that *"Managers"* do not have to be THE technical experts, but aggregators of people assets, technology and visions ... that work. The old models of *"barking"* Production Managers and reticent Office Managers will be gone. Their replacements will have the ability to Connect and Engage with others in a deep and meaningful way and to map a non-contentious path to desired outcomes.

Creativity and Innovation will be the focus of rewards and not just confined to a small group of pre-selected internal talent. As The Great Workplace 2.0 is now being built upon internal and external Collaborations, The Great Workplace 3.0 will take this to a new level with time to deployment being decreased. Effective channels of Creativity and Innovation will be boosted by web-based tools and external talent. The Great Workplaces will look for people who think out of their Three-Foot Circles, and will develop those who show promise, while maintaining open communications with those who are external. This development foundation will come from having created a culture that fosters creativity, but also encourages an environment that expects it. Collaborative engagement of all Participants, and the seeking of external Collaborations will become a standard of Operations. The Tools to achieve this are not only on the Internet, but are also available for Smartphone's and tablets. Many are disguised as *"Project Management"* software applications and *"White Boards"*.

Adaptable Business Model: Global and local organizations are seeking to minimize *"Positive Response Time"* to changing economies and world events that sway macro- and micro-markets. It is no longer acceptable to over-wait and analyze. Being swift to respond, or having already put into place viable alternative products or services, is becoming a value proposition with each organization and directly to Customers, who are reducing their own response time to their Customers. Small- to medium-size organizations are now seeing their size and lack of *"red tape"* as a marketing differentiator. This is changing their *"How."* In many cases their *"What"* (products/ services) are morphing as the markets dictate. Technology is being viewed as a proactive tool, not simply as a place-holder in their foundation.

Additive Manufacturing: 3-D printing or *"fast prototyping,"* typically done with polymers, metals or concrete in machines that *"Add"* layers of materials to build either prototypes, or where appropriate, small quantities of finished product. Time to turnaround: less than one day. To accomplish that same feat in metal machining, just the machine setup time could take days or weeks. This is a highly adaptive tool when customers need to feel that your response time is Remarkable. With your customers turning on their own dimes with their customers, this is a great *"How"* in your Purpose, and marketing efforts. (Remarkable)

Machines to do repetitive tasks, and more: This is not new, but the strategy to replace repetitive work done by people, is accelerating. Advanced manufacturing technology will have an impact on increasing, not decreasing unemployment as machines are replacing the middle layer of the unskilled workforce, leaving semi-skilled (before Trained Technical Skills) functions where base cognitive skills are being used and saving the lowest level 'brawn' jobs. More of the lower level brawn jobs will be supplied by interim or interim-to-direct workers, to balance workflows. This pushes the semi-skilled folks in a position to seek training and advance to a skilled level or get stuck (again). It is an ongoing choice for tomorrow's workforce: get training and education above subsistence level or lose your future. Eventually, the lower skilled jobs will (and are) begin to fade due to poor, base education levels and lack of job accountability (show up on time, show up at all, and actually work). Robotics design and manufacturing organizations are extremely busy now. Their entire field of technology is accelerating rapidly, and with the increasing frustration of their customers with the status quo of the lower level workforce.

As a personal statement born from professional observations, our high school educational system is becoming the bottleneck to an evenly shared economic future, especially in urban areas. Putting *"disadvantaged"* status aside, a huge push to motivate school systems to actually connect and engage students in preparation for future work is no longer just critical. The entire system needs to be broken, taken away from Administrators who received their degrees in education 20- to 40-years ago, taken away from Unions and put into the hands of *"Crisis Management"* specialists: The best of the Charter systems (albeit many Charter Schools are worse than Public schools), borrow the templates from successful urban school systems, whatever it takes. Our suburban systems work, for the most part, but they too need some nudging. Or, urban systems could be sold off to McDonalds or Wendy's food chains as that is where most graduates and drop-outs wind up anyhow. And yes, I am fully aware that *"Environment"* is an enormous weight on the shoulders of students, and consequently the education systems that serve them. There will always be a certain percentage of students who will fail, drop out and not *"get"* their need for a future, regardless of the curriculum and educator approach. And yes again, there is no easy solution, but asking the systems that created the current state of affairs to solve problems, simply makes no sense.

Educating the workforce beyond High School: Remarkable Organizations already realize the competitive advantage of having a trained and educated workforce, as difficult as it may be to acquire and retain. Astute organizations are now Partnering with Community Colleges, online universities and two- and four-year universities to bring needed skills to their Tipis. The gap between high-school education and the needs of The Great Workplaces today has reached a precarious level. High-school math, physics, reading and cognitive skills are at a new low and will continue to sink.

The gap between working middle class and working poor will continue to increase due to the widening gap in fundamental education that is accepted and applied. As organizations continue to advance the technology used in their base business models there will be an increased need for Participants to function with this technology and use cognitive skills to make sense of and give meaning to information. Lower paying jobs are beginning to fade at a faster rate while jobs using higher level skills developed through education and training will continue to grow. To achieve self-support in life, it is no longer acceptable to stop learning in the 9th grade.

Employers are now making direct connections and investments with skill training organizations to offer in-house learning opportunities and to send eager students out to learning centers. Employer groups (manufacturing in particular) have united association members in need of trained factory technicians to send the best and brightest student interns to advanced-technology training, and to hire graduates directly from those same institutions. The manufacturing community is directly advising on needed skills after graduation, and assuring their financial and knowledge support to those institutions.

Online education has even been created by The Great Workplaces themselves. Jergens, Inc. of Cleveland, Ohio has an in-house, online school called *"Tooling U"* that is helps train and develop skilled manufacturing technicians. This product started years ago as an in-house mechanism, and has proved itself in application so much so that it is offered as a product to other organizations. Jergens is NOT a large company like a G.E., so this is an example of being Remarkable: http://www.toolingu.com.

Free online courses are offered by top universities: Stanford, Berkeley, Cal, MIT, Harvard and more. The Faculty Project is a growing effort to bring professors from many top universities (USC, Duke, Dartmouth, Vassar, Northwestern, etc.) together in one location to offer free courses online (http://facultyproject. org/). Many courses are convertible to credit, most are the same classes given to enrolled, sitting students. Remarkable Organizations are finding that requiring online, advanced coursework supports and develops cognitive skills for chosen workers. The number of courses offered is increasing on a daily basis. And of course, online universities like Phoenix offer courses to a PhD level, for a fee.

In the past, organizations have offered tuition reimbursement to Participants desiring to continue their own education. In many ways this offering was not really *"pushed"* to employees, due to cost and the fact that organizations were losing trained employees to higher salary offers at the end of time-restrictive contracts. Today, with control of targeted courses for reimbursement this offered benefit is making a come-back.

The mission for Remarkable Organizations is to purposely develop their workforce, not wait for that to happen through hiring knowledge, or waiting for eligible workers to decide to pursue coursework on their own.

The Remarkable Organizations of The Great Workplace 3.0 take control of workplace skills and development on their own. It is, again, a competitive advantage as reflected in the core Values of the organization.

Data: Google already knows just about everything about you, your family, friends, customers, employees and other Participants to your success. So do Amazon, Target, Walmart and the government. They can "predict" what you will do and buy. The TV show *Person of Interest* takes that a step further using video, databases and public information.

Google knows every product that is manufactured and its specifications, as long as the company posted it to a website or someone has commented on it. Google knows everything about your customers. To tap into their knowledge in many paradigms, all you have to do is use Google Search. And there are more ways to mine Google data. Just ask them.

Forward-thinking organizations are now investing more in purchased, targeted data (existing and custom), organizing their own data into *"Actionable Knowledge"* pools and are mining those data pools for clues to future trends, buying habits and the need for innovative products or services. This is one junction where the new Medicine People will achieve high paybacks: Making sense of the data and applying the meanings that come from that. This will result in Actionable Knowledge: knowledge or data that has direct applicability to your issue or opportunity and can be used to make beneficial decisions.

Social media: If your organization is in a consumer-centric business, you need to master social media. In 2012-2013, we are still exploring the *"business value"* of social Connectivity. Most social media (public) is used by people for their own amusement, not on behalf of the organizations for which they work. Facebook is an example of this.

LinkedIn can be used effectively to promote and connect professional businesses to vendors, buyers and prospective talent, as well as to personally learn from and Collaborate with other professionals in your field or in fields you would like to research. Memberships in topical or affinity groups, where ideas and research are exchanged, can be a worthwhile endeavor. Twitter is a way of broadcasting brief statements of news and information links that expand to Internet-based articles of interest. The productive use of Twitter depends largely upon the nature of your business and the audience you wish to reach. Social media should be strategically applied with your Integrated Operating Plan and be connected to your website model.

Any business curious about the payback of social media should engage a professional consulting organization in this field. These organizations can guide your set up of an effective strategy, help develop and execute your plan and are also capable of providing content. A component of social media strategy will be linking your Collaborative processes (Virtual Collaborative Models), your data-mining and marketing strategies into one integrated system with effective subsystems. It is best to seek professional social media design and development organizations through your referral network.

Websites: The Great Workplaces don't let *"Tim,"* the college-age nephew, design and deploy a professional site, regardless of his apparent knowledge. Your Internet presence is not only your first impression given to Customers, vendors and prospective Talent; it is also how your industry will view you. Are you a player or are you a wanna-be? Effective sites are simple to navigate, content-rich (a visitor can learn from your site), dynamic in user interface (Remarkable user interface) and tell your *"story."* Prospective customers will look at your site before your sales representative visits on an appointment. The customer is looking to pre-discover the *"Why"* of considering you as a supplier. Your *"What"* (Products or services) should be clearly evident, but that is not enough. Your Purpose for the customer has to be clear, not mixed with your internal Missions (those are for you, not customers) and your Values need to be discoverable.

Potential Collaborators will make decisions on the extent and depth of their creative commitment to your organization based upon your evidence of having a public strategy for your market in place. Experts want to work with serious organizations, not take on the role of primary educators.

Prospective talent will look at how you promote your organization as a preferred workplace and how you encourage talent to inquire. For prospective talent, it is the place to begin your Immersion process and set up future hires for success.

The Great Workplaces 2.0 and 3.0 realize that the Internet is a connected and Collaborative Global Marketplace and approach their presence there with integrated strategy. They realize that this marketplace moves at the speed of light, gone are the days of large-scale mailings that take weeks and months to plan then execute. An online initiative reaches a massive audience in a click and garners feedback, if not sales, almost as fast. In many ways, this Collaborative, Integrated Marketplace is a zero-sum ballgame with only winners and losers among competitors.

Retail is changing the way they market to customers in-store. Video captures your *"profile"* (age, sex, produces ads of products you may want to buy and suggests alternatives or upgrades from RFID tags embedded in your selected products, even in the fitting rooms. Sci-Fi movie themes are no longer just for amusement. Amazon does the same thing while you are shopping online. As many new businesses are retailers in some fashion, the study of New Technology applications to your business, even if you cannot currently apply them today will begin to reshape your strategic plans for achieving your goals. It is important that your thinking is one step ahead of your reality. This alone can cement *"Enduring Organization"* in your Culture.

In the inevitable move to being The Great Workplace 3.0, the deployment of data and its analysis, tools, adaptable systems, increased and expanded Collaborations and the acquisition and development of the *"'New' Right People"* will define the ability to be Remarkable. The attempt only to be different without having built a secure foundation from the 13 Characteristics of **Remarkable**

Organizations will surely keep your organization in a permanent state of playing catch up with competitors in your market space. When everything described here becomes part of your Culture (*Values in Action*) you will be ahead of the game.

Be a Leader. Be Remarkable.

Would you like to become a contributor to The Great Workplace 3.0? I am looking for real-life stories. Tell me about yours. ras@thegreatworkplace.com

Pilamaya Tanka (Big Thank You).

Final Chapter
Creating The Great Workplace 2.0

"Curly's Rule"

Remember it? If not, Google it.

It's the only thing you really need to know.

"Ho, hecetu yelo."

About the Artist and Author

Bio – Valerie J. Evans

Valerie Evans is a self-taught artist who works primarily in colored pencil. Many of her paintings are a reflection of her own Native American heritage. She is an enrolled member of the Delaware tribe from Six Nations Reserve, Ontario, Canada. Ms. Evans prior experience includes serving as a police officer with the Ontario Provincial Police before moving to the United States, where she honed her skills as a portrait artist.

Valerie is a stalwart advocate for Indigenous people and is currently employed with the American Indian Education Center in Parma, Ohio, a non-profit center. Her role as community liaison allows her to work closely with members of the Native community in order to formulate a high-quality mental health service delivery model that is sensitive to our traditional spiritual and cultural values.

Her Native American Portrait series has been exhibited at Cleveland State University and Fra Angelica Gallery, located in Cleveland's Galleria Mall. It is permanently on display at the Peace Bridge Authority - Customs and Immigration Building in Fort Erie, Ontario. She also had the unique opportunity of exhibiting her artwork at the Cleveland Museum of Art during the *"Art of the Americas"* exhibition in 2010.

Ms. Evans resides in Westlake, Ohio with her husband and two children. She continues painting Native American subjects and welcomes commissioned portraits. She can be reached at valeriejevans@yahoo.com

Robert A. Schepens, CPC (Certified Personnel Consultant)

Robert has over 30-years experience in Human Resources, Recruiting, Staffing, Retained Search, Corporate Management and Business Ownership.

He bought his family's business, Champion Personnel System, Inc., in 1995. Champion was founded by Robert's father, Ralph A. Schepens, CPC in Cleveland in 1964. Robert developed it quickly as a multiple, award-winning organization (Weatherhead 100, North Coast 99, Business Success Award, Most Dependable Staffing Service in Central USA, OBWC Safety Awards, First Level II Drug Free Staffing Service in Ohio and an ISO 9001:2000 Registration). Over the last 49 years the organization has successfully worked with over 7,000 hiring organizations in Northeast Ohio, placed over 60,000 people and completed over 2 million interim and contract assignments.

Robert has served as the President of the Cleveland Association of Personnel Consultants, with the Ohio Association of Personnel Consultants and as a Board member of the National Association of Personnel Services.

For this deeply researched book, Robert met with over 500 of Northeast Ohio's CEOs and top Human Resource executives in small- to medium-sized privately or closely held organizations, consumed over 300 books on varying business topics plus over 300 world-class *"White Papers"* on the characteristics of successful businesses.

Robert is an active member of the Native American community in Northeast Ohio, having served for the last 20 years on Native American Organization boards, and having been named *"Man of the Year"* by the American Indian Education Center of Cleveland,

Ohio in 2005. He has also served on many not-for-profit and for-profit boards in the region.

Robert is an active member and the drum keeper of Fire River Singers (Pow Wow drum).

Robert earned a degree in Fine Arts from Christ College at Valparaiso University. He completed additional specialized studies at UCLA, John Carroll University and Cambridge University.

Robert is married to Margaret 'Marti' Douglas, an enrolled member of the Seminole Nation of Oklahoma and an active community volunteer. They live in Bainbridge, Ohio.

And on a good night, you may catch him jamming along on his guitar in a smoky Blues joint.